IT CAN BE EASY TO

PRESENT YOURSELF WITH IMPACT

All you have to do is learn the skills. And with this book, you're taking the first step toward attaining and maintaining a totally professional image.

Caryl Winter, a specialist in business communications, is a veteran of the corporate world. She knows what it takes to succeed and she shares with you *in one volume* everything she teaches in workshops, seminars, and courses at the UCLA School of Management, Labor, and Business.

This book is the single best investment you can make in your future.

PRESENT YOURSELF WITH IMPACT

Techniques for Success

CARYL WINTER

BALLANTINE BOOKS • NEW YORK

Contents

Expanded Contents

Presentation
Tips

PRESENT YOURSELF WITH IMPACT

I. Creating an Aura of Competency

Call me anything, but don't call me incompetent!

A True Story about Competency (Mine)

Several years ago I accepted a staff support position at a large medical center in California. This position required me to interact with administrative department heads, nurses, doctors, and health care professionals. I had had my fair share of business experience, but my hospital experience was limited to birth (already forgotten), one minor operation (too scared to notice my surroundings), and a handful of patient visits. Naturally, my new colleagues and co-workers had some reservations about my lacking hospital background—and so did I!

My immediate concern then, during my first days on the new job, was not to start cleaning up the backlog of work left by my predecessor, but rather to present myself as a competent professional who was willing to learn about the special needs of the hospital environment and could capably fulfill the functions of the position.

So I set my priorities in order and made these my first tasks:

- I developed an action plan, outlining my job objectives and their implementation dates.
- I met with all department heads and all other key staff to introduce myself and to make known my willingness to help solve existing problems.
- I developed reporting mechanisms for keeping others informed of the status of their requests.
- I assessed my department's internal procedures—and documented them.
- I reorganized internal controls and instituted follow-up mechanisms.
- I kept management informed of my activities through written weekly progress reports.

What I tried to show in those first few weeks was that I could make a valuable contribution to the organization, but I also realized a personal benefit: I had set the standard for what would be my general on-the-job behavior. Everyone had gotten a taste of my work style and found it palatable. . . . I had made a positive impact.

The Rationale Behind Presenting Yourself for Impact

You might be thinking that displaying your competency is nothing more than showing off, tooting your own horn, and advertising your capabilities. And you were taught not to do that.

Showing that you are competent is your own best self-advertisement, but it is not just for your own benefit. In fact, displaying your competency is a way of showing others that you can get done what has to be done and that you are willing to take responsibility for your actions.

We can communicate our competency through a variety of forms—written forms, such as memos and reports, activities summaries, and résumés; oral forms, such as the telephone, meetings, speeches, and interviews; clothing style; and follow-up techniques—in short, all the ways we present ourselves to others.

What we present, and how we present it, can sometimes make the difference between a one-time compliment or continued acceptance of our ideas. In some circles this is known as the "Masters and Johnson approach": It's not only *what* you deliver but *how* you deliver it that makes the impact!

And like the Masters and Johnson approach, skills for presenting yourself for impact can be learned—and practice is fun too! These presentation skills will strengthen your professional image, increase your organizational value, and perhaps even get you a new position. At the very least, though, you will reassess your feelings about yourself as a successful business communicator. So think again about tooting your own horn—you just might deserve it.

Essential Ingredients of Effective Presentations

As the teacher of an adult education college course entitled "Business Communications," the question I am asked most frequently is "Can you teach me how to make an effective presentation?"

My answer is "Yes, of course, if you realize that making an effective presentation requires more than just being a glib speaker or writing creative letters. Don't misunderstand me; these are certainly necessary ingredients, but they're just part of the pie."

And then I usually look out over forty alert faces, eager for me to bestow the divine answer. But I'd be a poor teacher if I just handed them the answer—and would you want me to give in so easily to you too?

Instead of giving you the answer so quickly, let me summarize how "top brass" feels about the subject of presentations. In an informal survey of top management personnel on what they want from a presentation, these comments were heard repeatedly*:

The Dirty Dozen: Management's Suggestions about Presentations

1. No excuses—give me action!
2. Don't tell me what I already know—tell me what I don't know and need to know.
3. Whatever the form—make it short and to the point.
4. Don't waste my time—be prepared and organized.
5. Give me information in a presentable form so that I can pass it along "as is" to others and don't have to spend my time doing it over.
6. Don't brag about how smart you are.
7. Tell me how I'll benefit from this presentation— tell me what's in it for me, not just what's in it for you.
8. Let me know that you're keeping on top of things.
9. Let some of your personal qualities come out— be natural.
10. Don't bore me with facts and statistics—hold my interest.
11. Keep me aware of the action on a regular basis.
12. Show me you can handle the assignment.

These are not necessarily listed in order of importance or frequency.

What conclusions can we come to about the components of effective presentations, after reading the Dirty Dozen list?

Components of Effective Presentations

- Preparation
- Organized information
- Complete information
- Consistency
- Willingness to accept responsibility
- Humor, lightness, and personality
- Lack of ego
- Competency

So what can we conclude:

1. An effective presentation is one that shows you are thoroughly prepared.
2. An effective presentation contains information that is organized in a complete and concise manner.
3. An effective presentation reveals your human side.
4. An effective presentation is a competent one—one that shows you have the skill and ability to carry out a particular assignment.
5. An effective presentation is one that keeps your audience aware of your actions in a consistent manner.

How a Steady Program of Consistent Communications Can Increase Your Success

A True Story about Consistency (Not Mine)

Adele was a contracts administrator at an insurance company. After learning about the advantages of progress reports in her business communications course, she began presenting her boss with a report of her activities at the end of each month. In due time, Adele was offered an advancement with another insurance company, and she accepted the new job.

After the first month on her new job Adele, from habit, prepared a progress report for her new boss. She explained what she had accomplished during that first month, what she proposed to do in coming months, and what kinds of changes she wanted to implement. Adele sent the report to her boss. He was extremely impressed with Adele's report; he'd never seen anything like it before, certainly not in his company. He was also impressed with Adele's initiative—she had made a presentation without anyone requesting it. He was so impressed in fact that Adele was given a raise!

Consistency certainly paid off for Adele, and it can work to your advantage as well, although not always with the guarantee of financial reward.

Another True Story about Consistency (Mine)

Remember that hospital job I told you about some pages ago? One of my duties was to keep the hospital supplied with an infinite variety of forms—all of the paperwork needed to support the day-to-day operations of the hospital.

The nature of the job was such that things always seemed to go wrong: Work couldn't be performed because a form was out of stock; schedules had to be rearranged because the right form wasn't available yet for use; people were using the wrong form because they didn't know a replacement existed; and so on. Complaints were so commonplace that people lined up outside my office to get their turn to scream at me.

Every day I faced a consistent fact: Some crisis would surely rear its nasty head. I didn't know if I could solve all of the crises, but at least I could let people know what I was doing to prevent them! So I began a program of sustained communication with my chronic complainers: I kept them informed of their projects' scheduled completion dates; I published status reports; I told them about problems as soon as I learned of them and suggested alternatives if possible; and I hand-carried items for approval. (They loved the personal service!)

Did I solve all my problems and make everyone happy? No way! But I did get a lot of "thank you's," and I did gain their confidence, and that made all our days easier. What pleased me the most was the feeling of relaxation we all experienced. They knew I was keeping on top of things, so their anxiety levels diminished. And when they relaxed, I could relax and concentrate my energies on making things run more smoothly—this helped them relax even more. But it couldn't have happened without a consistent program of open communication.

In my case, there was no financial reward; but my efforts paid off in greater confidence, renewed respect, and the achievement of my professional goals—and isn't that what success is all about?

Maintaining a Professional Image

However you present yourself—through verbal, written, and nonverbal means—the image you present to others and to yourself must be a true reflection of your competency.

So much has been written, televised, and argued about the subject of success (and its magic ingredients), but it all comes down to what you can *deliver consistently*—not just one time, not because of luck, but because you convey a true, steady assurance of your capabilities.

So the ground rules are simple:

Maintaining a Professional Image

1. Make sure your presentations reflect your competency.

2. Deliver consistently.
3. Keep your audience steadily assured of your capabilities.

Let's explore this concept in more detail, as we examine the variety of presentation methods available to us.

·························

II. Overview of Presentation Methods

Speak it, meet it, or write it—how do I choose?

Choosing Your Presentation Method

There is such a variety of presentation methods available today—no wonder we have trouble communicating!

A lady at a seminar I once gave shared her definition of *communication* with us, and I like it so much that I want to share it with you: "Communication is two-way understanding: Written communication is two-way reading; oral communication is two-way listening; nonverbal communication is two-way seeing."

What are some of the forms that communication takes these days?

Written Communication

- letters, memos, and reports
- business cards, brochures, and promotional literature
- résumés

Oral Communication

- telephone calls
- meetings or informal talks
- interviews
- sales presentations

Nonverbal Communication

- body language
- dress and personal grooming

Quite an assortment, isn't it? It's enough to drive a person crazy, especially with all the other responsibilities we have. And with all these options, how do we make the right decisions? Fortunately (I guess), we don't have any choice about nonverbal communication because it's always with us, whether we want it there or not; but is it sometimes better to put things in writing instead of saying them? And if you do choose to write, how do you know that it's written well?

And what about the argument that it takes too long to write—the telephone is handier?

And how do you conduct yourself at meetings, assuming you should go to them?

And how do you let people know you can be relied upon, that you're doing a good job?

And, and, and, and, and...the list is endless.

That's why in this book I will explore with you the various methods of communication and their possible consequences. Let's start with a bit of self-evaluation: Which communication methods do you prefer?

Test Your Business Communications Quotient (BCQ)

Circle the answer that most applies to your communication technique:

Seldom   Often   Never

1. Do you put things in writing, rather than handling them in person or by telephone?

2. Do you reach for the phone rather than write a memo?

3. Do you follow up on tasks and projects?

4. Do you tend to let things drop, once the responsibility has been assigned to another person?

5. Do you prefer to meet with someone to discuss a situation?

6. Do you avoid meetings?

7. Which means of communication do you favor?
   - letters, memos, and reports
   - telephone conversations
   - meetings

Interpretation of Your BCQ

Question	If You Circled	Interpretation
1. Put it in writing	Seldom	You are a people person and would rather go directly to the source; you find it quicker and easier to talk to people.
	Often	You pride yourself on your writing ability; you may prefer writing to the reality of dealing with people.
	Never	It probably takes you a lot of time to write; you may not have confidence in yourself as a writer.
2. Reach for the phone	Seldom	You enjoy the challenge of writing and like to give people something to refer to.
	Often	You are probably always running against time and need to get answers in a hurry; you think it takes too much time to write.
	Never	You may not have confidence in yourself as a verbal person.
3. Follow up	Seldom	You usually don't have time for follow-up, or you don't think of it as a worthwhile activity.
	Often	You see follow-up as a necessary and vital link in the communication

Question	If You Circled	Interpretation
		process; you probably have a reputation for competence with your colleagues.
	Never	You may be losing status with your colleagues for not keeping on top of things.
4. Let things drop	Seldom	You like to keep on top of things.
	Often	You may be a delegator, but be careful of becoming a dumper.
	Never	You tend to follow through, even after delegating responsibility.
5. Prefer meetings	Seldom	You may be wary of human interaction; you may not want to discuss all the other issues that can arise in face-to-face situations.
	Often	You like the personal interaction of meetings and don't mind dealing with any other issues that surface; you enjoy listening.
	Never	You prefer the one-sidedness of writing.
6. Avoid meetings	Seldom	You enjoy the give-and-take of ideas that occurs in meetings.

Question	If You Circled	Interpretation
	Often	You probably view meetings as taking too long and wasting your time; you usually have more important duties to attend to.
	Never	You view meetings as times of growth.
7. Favorite communication: letters, memos, and reports	Seldom or Never	You are probably a good talker, but you need to sharpen your written communication skills.
	Often	You like the impact of putting things in writing, but you may need to engage in more verbal situations.
telephone conversations	Seldom or Never	Get on the horn and talk to people.
	Often	Try documenting some of your talks, just for the record.
meetings	Seldom or Never	Get out there and interact with others.
	Often	Good for you, but keep written records of your discussions.

You Are What You Project

So now you can see yourself as a writer, a phoner, or a meeter. It's usually a surprise to find out about your true communication style, and you may or may not be happy with your findings.

Hold on, though, we're not through. Communication style has to be examined from another side—the receiver's side! It's not enough to communicate according to your own style; you must ask yourself "What method of communication does my receiver prefer?"

Aha! Maybe that's why you don't get answers to your memos—your receiver likes verbal requests. Or maybe that's why the meeting didn't go well—your receiver prefers to study written documentation.

So what conclusion can we make about choosing a method of communication? In order for a message to be communicated to another, it must be presented in the communication style preferred by the receiver.

Understanding the Art of Getting Your Point Across

The ability to convey ideas clearly, completely, quickly, and confidently—that's what communication is all about. You may not always be able to have your ideas accepted, but there should never be any doubt about what message you are trying to get across.

Let's take these concepts one at a time:

1. Convey your ideas clearly:
   • Plan what you want to say.
   • Use language your audience can understand.

- Present your information in a logical sequence.
- Make your ideas easy to understand.

2. Convey your ideas completely:
   - Cover all your information.
   - Anticipate negatives, criticism, and rejection—and be ready to respond.

3. Convey your ideas quickly:
   - Get to the point and stay on it.
   - Say what you have to say . . . and then end it.

4. Convey your ideas confidently:
   - Be natural—let your personality come through.
   - State your information in positive terms.
   - End your presentation with an action item.

So 1 + 2 + 3 + 4 = Getting Your Point Across.

Getting your point across is an art, but it's one that can be learned and perfected.

Another important component of getting your point across is that the information should be presented from the receiver's point of view. Ask yourself these questions:

- How will the receiver benefit from this presentation?
- How can I present this information so that the receiver can gain from it?

In planning how you are going to get your point across, you must ask *not*: What do I want to say? *but*: What does my receiver want to hear?

Communication, then, must not be self-directed but other-directed; it should be external rather than internal; and it should focus on "you" rather than "me."

How to Get Your Point Across

1. Convey your ideas clearly, completely, quickly, and confidently.

2. Present your information from the receiver's point of view.

Verbal or Written Communication?

We move fast these days, and we usually need information in a jiffy—to answer a question, to help with a decision, to plan a course of action, to get things moving. And we usually expect that information to be at someone's fingertips; otherwise we find ourselves "on hold" and the process comes to a halt again.

The Telephone

The telephone is an informal way of conveying or requesting information, usually in a one-to-one situation (let's put aside telephone conference calls for the time being). That's why the telephone is such a vital tool to the business communicator. The telephone is likely to be used for these kinds of situations:

- I need this information, and I need it now.
- Here's the answer you wanted.
- Let's discuss a situation.
- I want to make an appointment.

The decision to use the telephone is often based on speed and informality, but it's also used in situations where a resolution can be easily reached. In other words, the telephone is used for self-limiting situations.

Meetings

The other forms of verbal communications—meetings, informal talks, interviews, and presentations—often are more formal because they're usually prearranged for a specific time, all parties agree to the "interruption," and information can be presented to and shared among multiple parties.

Some formal meetings are documented in the form of minutes, but for most informal meetings there is no record of the conversation or the decisions made. What was said circulates in the air and the mind, and we can only hope that the right information made its mark and lingers in the mind.

Writings

If you want to reach a number of parties with hard-core information and have evidence of your ideas, then the written format is for you. You and your readers will have a permanent reference record of all that was presented.

The written format is the best means of communication when you have a lot of information to be transmitted. Putting it down on paper can also help to sharpen clear-thinking skills—yours as well as your receiver's.

Written words can also be used to convey good news, to confirm a decision, to outline what was verbally discussed, to add a friendly touch, and to create a strong impression. After all, it takes time and effort to write (anyone who has ever struggled with a letter or memo knows that), and we all appreciate someone putting time in on our behalf. There is, after all, an extra impact made when you take the time to convey your ideas in writing.

If you're still debating about whether or not to put your thoughts in writing, ask yourself these questions:

• Should I make the time for writing?
• Do we need documentation?
• Will I make a greater impact if I put my ideas in writing (often in addition to the oral presentation)?

If you answered any of these questions positively, then my advice is to put it in writing.

Summary of Communications Methods

Telephone

- An informal way of conveying information
- Usually in one-to-one situations
- When speed is a factor
- When resolutions can be swiftly reached

Meetings

- More formal way of conveying information
- Information usually shared among multiple parties
- Sometimes documented in the form of minutes

Writings

- A formal way of reaching one or more parties with information
- When documentation is desirable and necessary
- Conveys a commitment because of the time and effort it takes to prepare words

Speak It, Meet It, or Write It?—The Choice Is Yours

In making your decision about the means of communication, consider these factors:

How to Choose a Communications Method

Questions to Ask Yourself	If You Answer "Yes," Choose This Method
1. Do I need information immediately?	Speak it

2. Do I have information to present
   to multiple parties?   Meet it or Write it

3. Do we need documentation?   Write it

4. Do we need two-way
   communication?   Speak it or Meet it

5. Do I want to make a special
   impact?   Write it

When you've chosen your method(s) of communication, you can move on to the next important task: strategy planning.

· ·

III. Strategy Planning

What do I want to accomplish?

Choosing the Appropriate Strategy

You've made your decision about whether your presentation will be a verbal or written one. Good. But before you reach for the phone, your dictating machine, or your yellow pad, ask yourself: What do I want my presentation to accomplish?

You see, you have to define your purpose so you'll know how to tackle the issues. In other words, if you don't know what you want to accomplish, then how can you possibly do it? Defining the purpose is the most essential ingredient in helping you make an effective presentation. Effective presentations don't just happen haphazardly; rather, the good ones are always carefully thought out in advance.

Developing an Effective Presentation

There are four steps in developing a presentation. When you master the dynamics, you too will be a POPP star.

How to Be a Presentation POPP Star

1. <u>P</u>lan
2. <u>O</u>rganize
3. <u>P</u>repare
4. <u>P</u>resent

What's involved in each of these steps?

Planning: deciding on your objective; identifying your audience; and choosing a suitable strategy.

Organizing: setting your priorities in order; deciding what specific information to cover; staying on the track.

Preparing: putting it all together; doing a test run; anticipating requests, barriers, or objections.

Presenting: giving it your best shot; calling for action; requesting feedback.

Planning + Organizing + Preparing + Presenting will make you a Popp star.

Let's examine each of these aspects in some detail.

Step 1—Planning Your Presentation

When we plan our presentation, we usually think about the way in which we hope to obtain our goal. But we must also identify that goal. Planning, then, encompasses several stages.

Stage 1: Decide on your objective for the presentation.

- Do you want to present information?
- Do you want to make a request?
- Do you want to call attention to a problem?
- Do you want to make a recommendation?
- Are you calling for a course of action?
- Are you trying to present a convincing argument?
- Are you trying to sell your abilities?

You can, of course, have a combination of objectives; the trick is to identify them so they don't take you or your audience by surprise.

Which leads us to the next part in planning your presentation.

Stage 2: Identify your audience and your audience's preferences.

- Does your audience like to read this kind of material or to see and hear it?
- Is your audience interested in numbers, cost savings, innovative techniques, historical background, or people?
- Is your audience conservative or progressive in background or outlook?
- Is your audience easy or tough to convince?
- How much time can your audience contribute to this presentation?
- Do you have competition for this presentation (other people, time factors, cost constraints)?
- What is your relationship to your audience (nonexistent, personal, professional)?

When you have identified these two parts of the planning process—when you know your objective and your audience—you can proceed to the next stage.

Stage 3: Choose a suitable strategy.

- What is the best way to convince your audience (with figures, examples, or results; by making specific recommendations; by exhibiting competency)?
- Can your audience tolerate a lighter, humorous approach?
- How will your audience benefit from this presentation?
- What is your audience's bottom line—what will convince your audience?
- What need can you fulfill?

Planning your presentation will save you a lot of second-guessing and unnecessary aggravation later, when it's too late and the opportunity has passed.

Step 2—Organizing Your Presentation

After you have identified your objective, audience, and strategy, you can proceed to the next step: getting organized.

Stage 1: Set your priorities in order.

- Make a list of the main ideas or categories you need to cover.
- Group similar ideas together so that your list begins to develop some order.
- Arrange your groupings in priority order, according to urgency, importance, or time frame, and then number them (1, 2, 3, 4 or A, B, C, D).

Stage 2: Decide what specific information to cover.

- Take each main idea or category and list the points that could be treated within that category.
- Examine each point and ask yourself, "Does this illustrate, support, or enhance my overall objective(s)?"
- Eliminate the unnecessary or irrelevant points.
- Continue this process for each main idea or category, until your list contains only the most pertinent and relevant items.

Once you have condensed it all, you will feel much more in control of your material. Before you will be ready to make a really impressive presentation, however, you need to go through one more stage:

Stage 3: Stay on the track.

- For each point you want to include, ask yourself the big question: "Is it worth my and my audience's time?"
- When your answer is no, think again about the particular point—modify it or eliminate it for a better presentation.
- When your answer is yes, then you know you're on the right track.

Now you're ready. You have prepared a game plan—and that's what separates an effective presentation from an ordinary one. The amount of organizational groundwork you lay before actually starting the presentation can help smooth the way to success. When you have planned and organized, you have completed the hardest tasks in making a presentation.

And now, because you have mastered the most restricting parts, your reward is to be able to move on to the fun parts: to test your strategy and to enjoy the pleasures of making an effective presentation.

Step 3—Preparing Your Presentation

Preparing your presentation is very much like a dress rehearsal. In fact, if it's a visual presentation you're making, you most certainly should include a "dress test." But let's not jump to that stage just yet.

Now it's time to take all the information you've thought about, collected, and mulled over, and tie it neatly together to see how well it fits.

Stage 1: Put it all together.

- "Write" your presentation.
  —If it is to be a *written* presentation, then string your

information together in the proper format.
—If it's an *oral* presentation, put all your facts together
and examine them.
—If it's a *visual* presentation, get your outfit and your
supplies together.
• Think about the impact your presentation will make on
your audience.

Stage 2: Do a test run.

• Share your presentation with someone—a trusted colleague, a supportive yet critical spouse, an unbiased
coworker—in short, someone who can look at the presentation from a critical distance and evaluate it from your
and your audience's point of view.
• Try your presentation on yourself: read it aloud, stand
before a mirror, examine yourself with a critical eye.
• Accept the strokes and criticism—and refine your presentation, if necessary.

Once you have put your presentation together, gotten
some reaction, and modified your actions accordingly, there
is one more step before facing your audience: You need to
develop some awareness of the objections you might encounter so that you can prepare yourself to meet them and
to address them positively. This is known as "being on top
of your game."

Stage 3: Anticipate requests, barriers, or objections.

• Think about any possible shortcomings or limitations in
your presentation.
• Anticipate problems or objections or requests.
• Be prepared to address these roadblocks so that you are
not taken by surprise when you learn of some objections.
• Formulate your advance answers in positive tones, rather
than in negative defensive ways—stress what you can do
rather than what you can't do.

Finally . . . the moment you have been so patient about: Presenting yourself with impact.

Step 4 — Presenting Yourself

This is your time to shine, your chance to show yourself to others as the star you know you are!

Stage 1: Give it your best shot.

- Present the most professional package you can create, taking into consideration your audience's priorities, your objectives, and the information at hand.
- Enjoy yourself while making your presentation; present confidence and helpfulness.
- Come prepared as a team member, so that what you show reflects your willingness to be flexible.
- Make your presentation worth everyone's time.
- Present yourself with impact . . . or else why bother?

Now back up a bit . . . think again about your original reason for the presentation: your objective. This brings us to the next stage.

Stage 2: Call for action.

- End your presentation with an action item.
- Make a request of your audience, or state what you will do (depending upon who is carrying the responsibility).
- Be prepared with an action plan. It's not enough to state what must or will be done; you also have to know how to implement the plan.
- Follow through on your words; make sure that whatever was supposed to have happened does in fact happen. Now you start to get a reputation for reliability and competency and for being a results-getter — and that's what counts!

You've made your presentation. How do you know if it was effective? We can usually know that a presentation has been effective by the level of response it generates:

No response:	Perhaps the message wasn't communicated properly (or at all), or the action to be taken was not clear.
Negative response:	Perhaps the message was communicated, but the method or the information was not acceptable to the audience.
Positive response:	You did it!—No explanation needed.

We can't always assume that our audience will offer a response (even no response can be considered a response); sometimes you, the presenter, will have to specifically request one.

That's why this next stage is so important—you need to know if your presentation has been effective.

Stage 3: Request feedback.

- Make a specific request—by time or date, by action, by person.
- Hold up your end; follow through when necessary.
- Ask your audience for their honest opinion of your presentation, especially when you are trying out new or different techniques.
- Modify your next presentation, based on the feedback you receive.

So there you are: a Popp star! Let's summarize the requirements of the job.

How to Develop an Effective Presentation

1. Plan Your Presentation
   - Decide on your objective.
   - Identify your audience.
   - Choose a suitable strategy.

2. Organize Your Presentation
   • Set your priorities.
   • Decide on specific information.
   • Stay on the track.

3. Prepare Your Presentation
   • Put it all together.
   • Do a test run.
   • Anticipate requests, barriers, or objections.

4. Present Yourself
   • Give it your best shot.
   • Call for action.
   • Request feedback.

You now have the basic foundations for exhibiting your competency through effective presentations. Are you ready for a bit of self-examination?

The Presentation Quiz

1. I present only the necessary information.

2. I present myself clearly and succinctly.

3. I succeed in selling my ideas.

4. My letters, memos, and phone calls are answered.

5. I get responses to the methods through which I present myself.

6. I get feedback from my presentations.

7. I enjoy the presentations I make.

8. I leave a positive imprint through my presentations.

How many yes answers did you have? If you're not satisfied with your score, take the quiz again after you've

had the benefit of some clear instruction and positive re-
inforcement. The next chapters will show you how to present
yourself — for the various kinds of communications methods
and for the typical situations you'll encounter.

IV. Written Presentations

Forget your ego and just get on with it!

True Confession Time Again

An astute student recently asked me if it's easy for me to write. I told her it's easier, but it's not easy. And that's the most I can promise you: It will get easier, and at some point it might even start to become enjoyable. But it will take time, and because we associate time with work we think of writing as work.

I won't lead you astray: Writing is hard work, but the finished product can be so satisfying. When you reach the stage where you receive compliments on your writing, you'll be glad you took the time to write.

A well-written memo makes for good reading. And good reading is damn difficult writing. Does this sound as if I'm talking in circles? Travel with me through the process and product of writing—I'll show you how easy it can be.

The Elements of Readable Writing

Why do you want to write?

• To reach other people
• To make your position clear
• To promote understanding
• To transfer information
• To provide documentation

And how are you going to write?

• In a style and format understood by the reader.

Sounds simple, doesn't it? For many of us, things fall apart between the "wanting to write" and "going to write" stages. What gets in the way, I think, are the misconceptions we have about how business writing is supposed to sound. Let me dig back into my own past to tell you about my first encounter with these misconceptions; perhaps you share some of them.

I was hired for a summer job with a major financial giant in New York City. This was my first "real job" and I wanted to do my best. My duties were to verify account holders' names against a master list and then to write to those whose accounts had been inactive, whose whereabouts were in question, or whose accounts had problems.

The verification part of my job was easily accomplished, but the thought of writing letters put me in a panic state: How to write? What to say? Which things to mention? So I asked my supervisor for guidance, and she pulled out a hefty-sized notebook with sample letters requesting every conceivable combination of facts. My life was saved—all I had to do was fill in the different names, numbers, and amounts.

Back at my desk, I examined the letters and found them full of such statements as "Enclosed please find," "the afore-mentioned documents," "attached herewith," and "awaiting your reply." I had never used these statements in ordinary speaking, and I couldn't believe I'd have to use them in writing. Why couldn't I write a letter that sounded natural to me (and to my reader, I assumed)? So I did—but first I discussed it with my supervisor.

Our discussion revealed some long-standing myths, and I countered with some truths of my own:

Myth 1: Business writing is different from business conversation.
Truth: Business letters can be written in a conversational
style.

Myth 2: Business letters must contain formal expressions
that are not part of the writer's everyday vocabulary.
Truth: Business letters should contain words that are part
of the writer's regular vocabulary.

Myth 3: Business letters must not contain such common
forms as contractions, personal pronouns, and
names.
Truth: Business letters should be personal—what can be
more personal than names, personal pronouns, and
commonly used contractions?

Myth 4: Business letters should show off the writer's ability
to construct involved thoughts and sentences.
Truth: Business letters should be written to communicate—in the easiest possible way.

Myth 5: Business letters should show the writer's distance
from the reader and should express a master/servant
relationship.

Truth: Business letters should show the writer's and the
reader's involvement with each other.

My request to write more natural-sounding letters was
accepted, and I certainly felt more comfortable about writing
business letters from then on. Was I asking for something
impossible? Not at all.

The trend in business writing these days is to blend the
oral and written languages so that we don't have different
ways for writing and speaking. Otherwise we set up barriers
for ourselves and our readers.

It has been written that modern business writing should
be written to express, not to impress; I have no quarrel with
that. It has also been written that we should write the way
we speak. Here's where I begin to hear some hesitation,
some snickers, and to have some doubts myself. Haven't
these authorities ever heard of slang, story-telling, or off-
the-record stuff? What does it mean to write the way you
speak?

Writing the way you speak means two things: to use
language that will communicate with and speak to your
reader. The language you use should be part of your regular
vocabulary, and not just words that you use in a report to
impress the boss. If you write a word that is not commonly
part of your oral vocabulary, then it really doesn't belong
in any letter, memo, or report that you write. So use simple
words, words that your reader can read and understand.
After all, your aim is to communicate in the shortest way
possible; and we can usually do that best when we use simple
and easy-to-understand words.

Uh oh! I've probably hit a nerve. You're saying, "Well,
if I do that won't I sound like a sixth-grader? Won't I be
talking down to my reader?"

Aha! the magic words—*your reader*. So let's formulate

another truth: Write in language your reader can understand, and use technical terms and trade jargon *only* if your reader has knowledge of the terminology.

The other aspect of writing the way you speak is this: Write in a conversational style, as if the reader and you are sharing a conversation. That should give your writing a more natural flow and will help you keep the length of your sentences down to a pronounceable, breathable number.

Pronounceable? Who pronounces a written document? Don't you read it? No . . . we read documents aloud silently. I know that sounds like a paradox, but listen to yourself right now reading these words. You're doing it. And you pause and question and emphasize, just as if you were delivering a dramatic reading. How many words can you "pronounce" without having to take a breath? That's why in writing you need to keep the words in your sentences down to a workable number, so that your reader can understand the sentence thought and can "say" it without gasping for air. An average sentence length of about fifteen to twenty words is what your reader can accommodate. Use words that your reader will be able to read, understand, and accept upon the first reading.

As I mentioned before, your aim in writing is to have your written words sound just like your spoken words. Instead, what we usually do is think about what we want to say and then translate it into more formal-sounding businessese and write the translation on paper. Our reader gets the document, reads it, and says, "What the hell does this mean?" And then rereads and translates the words *back* to the writer's original thoughts. What we have is the writer and the reader doing the same thing: translate, write, read, translate—two parties doing double work. And what you've done is to create a negative feeling on the reader's part; anytime a reader has to stop to figure out what the words mean, the writer gets negative credibility points.

So make it easy for the reader to read and understand the first time around, without making it hard work.

Think also about the amount of time your reader can invest in reading and understanding your words. Condense your information down to the essentials. Pick out the important points from the extraneous ones and cover only the necessary ones.

We writers tend to think of our readers as our captives; that they will read every one of our words because our words are pearls. But when was the last time you read every word in a memo? Most memos are long-winded and repetitious. Worse, the important facts are usually buried among other facts and we have to pick them out. It's kind of like eating a lobster—you have to pick through a lot in order to get to the tasty part.

Make it easy for your reader to pick out the important parts. You can set these ideas apart from others by making them subject headings, for example, or by underlining them for emphasis, or by grouping them in a summary paragraph called "Important Points." What you're aiming for is some *visual* way of calling your reader's attention to those items worth studying.

Subject headings also serve another purpose, besides calling attention to important parts: They help you organize and keep you on an organized path. You can use headings to help you form an order for information—they give shape to your writing.

To sum up:

How to Write to Be Read

1. Write in a style and format that can be understood by the reader.
2. Use words that are part of your regular thinking and speaking vocabulary.
3. Make your writing personal: Use names, personal pronouns, and contractions.

4. Write to communicate—in the easiest possible way.
5. Show your interest in the reader.
6. Write to express, not to impress.
7. Write in simple words and short sentences.
8. Use technical terms and business jargon *only* if your reader is familiar with the terminology.
9. Use words that your reader will be able to read, understand, and accept upon the first reading.
10. Avoid the translation step—for you and your reader.
11. Pare your information down to the essentials.
12. Set off important information with subject headings, underlinings, or summary paragraphs.

Developing a Reader Attitude— the Human Touch

Some years ago I worked at a large insurance company that conducted most of its business by mail. Consequently the company was most concerned about the quality of its written communications.

Their concern was well-founded, because in a study of the public's feelings about the letters they received, four words kept reappearing. People believe business writing is:

1. cold
2. inconsiderate
3. authoritative
4. hard to understand.

In other words, business writing is all one-sided—from the writer's point of view. What remedies can we provide for our readers to change their opinions about business writing?

First off, put yourself in the reader's place rather than operating from your own point of view. Most of the time we write from that position: I want you to do this; we found this mistake; we need these things to happen. Well, what does the reader think: What about ME? What will I get out of it?

When you turn your orientation around so that you take the reader into consideration, your reader will be on your side, with you rather than against you.

And if you think of communication as a way of reaching people so that they can be shown how they can gain, then you are really increasing your own worth, getting people to go along with your ideas, and making a lot of friends along the way.

There's another myth: Business writing shouldn't be friendly; it should be stiff, formal, and distant-sounding. What I'd like to help you understand is that business writing can and *should* be friendly, or maybe *personal* is a more acceptable word. Always remember that you are communicating with another person, even if your message is being composed and transmitted through ultramodern electronic technology.

I think this explanation should help to eliminate the No. 1 and No. 2 no-no's from your writing. What about No. 3: the authoritative style?

Authority can usually be detected by such words as: *you will, we should, you must.* How can we soften the words but still get our reader to comply with the request? I just did it . . . by phrasing the request as a question. For example:

Instead of: You must sign this form and return it to us by the deadline of February 15 or else your automobile coverage will lapse.

How about: Can you please sign and return this form by

> February 15? That way you will be continu-
> ously insured.

Same idea, different approach. Which one would *you* respond to?

Sometimes readers need to feel that they have a choice in the matter rather than hearing definitive directives, so that the decision is in their hands. It's the attitude you take toward your reader that makes the difference.

And what about that underused word in the example: *please*? Won't you please use it more often?

Another approach to take to soften the authoritative style is to state what both parties will do, to show cause and effect:

> If you sign the form and return it by February 15,
> we'll be glad to continue your automobile coverage.

Thus both parties are equally involved. And when we're involved we communicate. Which brings us to No. 4 . . .

How can we communicate if our reader finds us hard to understand? We can't! Instead, we promote negative feelings because the reader feels uninformed, not so smart, and insecure. What we've done when we write for ourselves and not for our readers is to hammer home our own superiority. Big deal! Who cares how many technical terms you know and how many thoughts you can string together? Because if the reader says, "I don't understand what this is all about," then it's an empty battle the writer has won.

Remember, we're writing to express, not to impress! Before I forget—make sure you take out the garbage. What? You think I've gone crazy and confused a household chore with writing? Actually, they have a similar basis: Get rid of all the unnecessary stuff. Cut your thoughts to the bone—

you want to keep your reader from having to chew through the fat.

Give your reader all that's needed to know—no more, no less. Think about your reader's time, knowledge, and information needs; that should help you determine what to leave in, what to take out. Think about what your reader wants to know; that should help you in your approach to the subject. And your approach should be written from the reader's perspective with a positive attitude, because getting the reader on your side is more important than showing how much work you did. How can you get the reader on your side? By formulating and concentrating on your objective.

How to Identify Your Objective

Think about why you have decided to write or need to write. What do you want your message to accomplish? What do you want your reader to know or be able to do after reading your words? That's your objective. So why do we run into trouble? Usually because we begin our message with a history rather than with a purpose; or because we start to get the words down without thinking through our purpose. And when we work that way we're working without any direction.

Try this simple technique: On a piece of paper or an index card or whatever is handy, write the words "Why am I writing?" and then fill in the answer. Prop the card in front of you to help you formulate your opening—because your objective should be stated in your opening. It doesn't always have to be your first sentence (think how boring it would be to have all your messages begin "The purpose of this report is . . ."), but it should certainly be stated in your first paragraph.

How to Get Organized and Stay Organized

Which is harder: identifying your objective for writing or getting organized? Most hands will stay raised for organization. I think that's because of the way we were taught to write.

Most of us were taught how to write years ago in elementary school. We were instructed that everything we wrote should have three parts: an introduction, a body, and a conclusion; so we wound up saving the best for last.

And we learned how to make an outline, complete with Roman numerals, capital *A*'s and lower case *a*'s, and 1, 2, 3's. I remember frantically trying to think of a *b*, because I was warned that an outline couldn't have just an *a*.

And oh, that horrible homework assignment of having to write an outline and its fleshed-out report. I confess! I did it in reverse order. How many of you are in my club?

I'd like to recommend that we bury the outline and in its place substitute organized notes. My theory works like this:

How to Get Organized

1. Concentrate on your purpose for writing; write your purpose on a separate piece of paper or an index card; prop it in front of you.
2. Jot down at random all the points you need to cover.
3. Reread your list of points. See if any belong with any others; if so, group them together (you can use a symbol such as * or • or # to join similar ideas).

4. Look for a shape, an order of ideas. Prioritize your ideas and arrange them in sequence *according to your purpose for writing*. This is most important, because your purpose will help you keep on the track of what should be covered first, second, and so on.
5. End with an action item, an idea that you want to remain in your reader's mind; this will usually tie in with your reason for writing.

What you accomplish with this method is to begin with a purpose and end with that purpose. So in effect you will have come full circle and so will your reader—and that's organization!

This method should certainly take you less time than writing an outline would; it will help you get some skill in organizing your ideas and keeping on the track; and it should also keep you from overwriting and your reader therefore from having to plow through unnecessary information. And these days we can't be frivolous with reading and writing time, not with the business reality that time is money.

In this first section I have tried to present you with the basics for business writing. In these next sections we'll examine the various forms business writing takes these days: letters, memos, reports, progress reports, minutes of meetings. And we'll get some good tips on how to write for impact.

Effective Writing Tips

1. Develop a reader attitude:
   • Put yourself in the reader's place.
   • Try to reach the reader.

- Be friendly and personal, rather than authoritative.
- Give the reader alternatives.
- Make it easy for the reader to understand your message.
- Write to express, not impress.
- Give your reader all the information necessary.
- Be positive.

2. Identify your objective:
   - Think about what you want your message to accomplish.
   - Write a note to yourself saying, "Why am I writing?"
   - Prop the note in front of you and keep it there as a reminder of your purpose.
   - Begin with your purpose, not a history.

3. Get organized and stay organized:
   - Concentrate on your purpose for writing.
   - Make a list of the points to be covered.
   - Group similar points together.
   - Look for an order—arrange your ideas in priority sequence, according to your purpose for writing.
   - End with an action item.

Letters

A business letter is a written message, sent from one person to another person or to an organization. A business letter usually passes through the hands of the post office—as opposed to an interoffice memo, which is sent between people in the same organization via the interoffice mail system.

A business letter has two basic functions: to convey a message from the writer to the reader, and to give the reader a favorable impression of the writer and the writer's organization.

Sounds simple enough. So why do we sometimes write or receive letters that have unclear messages or that leave less-than-desirable impressions, especially when that wasn't the writer's intention? Because the writer usually doesn't look at the letter from the receiver's viewpoint. The writer knows what to say (the facts), why to say it (the reasons), but very often not how to say it (the approach). And the writer's approach can sometimes make all the difference between an unclear failure and a clearly written success.

How to Write Letters That Get Results

The concept of writing from the reader's point of view is known as the "you" approach—"you" refers to the reader, not the writer, of the message. (This is not a new technique I'm recommending here; it's been a staple of writing classes for many years.)

The "you" approach is easy to understand and easy to illustrate: Put yourself in the other person's shoes. Don't talk *to* him or her from your point of view with your concerns first; talk *with* your reader from his or her point of view with his or her concerns first.

Start utilizing the you approach right from the beginning of the letter, because that's the first thing the reader reads. Those opening words can make or break a friendship. After all, we are writing for others, not for ourselves.

Let's look at some startling facts about business letters:

- The cost of a business letter is over $7.00—and that's based on the writer/stenographer/typist method.
- It can take anywhere from five minutes to an hour for the author to compose a letter, but the reader reads it in less than a minute.

- Letters of more than one page immediately put off the reader because of their length.
- A business letter serves as the first and sometimes only means for making an impression on the reader.

What can we conclude from these facts? Since business letters are necessary but costly items, we had better get our reader involved at the beginning and our message across in the shortest possible time . . . or we may not get another chance to show our competency.

How are we going to get our reader involved and our message across?

- Write from the reader's point of view. This will help you write a more forceful letter.
- Use simple nontechnical language so your meaning will be perfectly clear and understandable to the reader; use short words and short sentences (fifteen to twenty words).
- Project a positive attitude. Tell your reader what you can do, rather than what you can't do. We are all turned off by negative statements, especially as opening statements.
- End your letter with a specific meaningful request or specific action: the "hot potato" technique.

The "hot potato," or action item, technique is a means of ending a letter with a clear understanding of what the next step is. Both writer and reader know into whose court the action has moved (the potato). The idea is to always end with a hot potato so that the person will have to get rid of it rather than get burnt. The hot potato will always cause some reaction, a movement. And, after all, aren't we writing letters to get results?

So say good-bye to such indefinite ending statements as:

- If you have any questions, please don't hesitate to call. (Who ever hesitates?)
- Awaiting your reply. (So wait!)

- Please return this at your earliest convenience. (That's after everything else.)

Instead, go for the exact:

- I'll call you next week to answer any questions this letter may have raised.
- Can we hear from you by April 15?
- As soon as we receive the signed documents, we'll be able to process a refund.

These four points will help you write better letters, so to sum up:

How to Write Letters for Results

1. Use the "you" approach.
2. Use simple, nontechnical language.
3. Project a positive attitude.
4. End with a hot potato.

Let's put these new skills to work. Here's the first exercise:

As the credit manager of a novelty items company, Elliott must approve the credit for all orders. The company's customers are mainly "mom and pop" gift shops and small-business owners. They will place a first order for merchandise and wait for the order to arrive. The company's policy is to gather credit information on these shop owners before any orders can be shipped. This is the standard letter Elliott's company sends to all new customers:

In order for us to approve this first order, a credit investigation will have to be conducted. Please fill out the enclosed credit application and return it to the undersigned. You will be contacted later regarding the results of this investigation.

What's wrong with this letter?

- It makes no attempt to establish good feelings with the customer.
- It makes no explanation as to why credit must be checked, thus creating confusion for the customer.
- It has no explanation about what happens to the order in the meantime.
- It is written from the company's point of view, not the customer's.
- It uses cold words such as *the undersigned* and *investigation*.
- It has only one reference to "you."

Take a stab at rewriting the letter from the "you" approach.

_____
_____
_____
_____
_____
_____

Here's my attempt:

   We appreciate your recent order for two dozen granny goose lamps; they will be a big seller for you. We'll be glad to ship your order as soon as we receive some credit information—this is standard procedure for all our new customers.

   Would you mind completing the enclosed appli-

cation and returning it to me? As soon as your credit
has been cleared, your lamps will be on their way.

Maybe my version isn't too terrific, but it certainly is an
improvement of the original letter:

- It attempts to establish good feelings between the customer
  and the company.
- It explains why a credit check is necessary.
- It explains that the order will be shipped when credit is
  cleared.
- It uses six "you" references and many personal pronouns.
- It has a warm friendly tone.

Can you see the difference the "you" approach can make
in your business letters?

Opening and Closing Statements

In the opening of our letter we want to get our reader
involved, and in our closing we want to describe the next
step. So what our reader reads first must make a favorable
impression, and what our reader reads last should give a
sense of what to do next. In between, the facts are stated.
Usually we don't have much trouble explaining the facts,
but our beginnings and endings could use some sprucing
up.

So many letters begin in the same old tired way; the most
commonly used are "Thank you for your letter of October
19," and "Enclosed please find the brochures you requested," and "In checking our records we found that our
invoice #3260 is still outstanding." (And so is that opening!)

Let's give some life to our writing, and certainly to our
readers. We write the same boring things; they have to read
the same boring things. So let's see how we can put some
life into these openings.

Boring	*Spruced Up*
Thank you for your letter of October 19 in which information was requested regarding an IRA account.	Here are the answers to your questions about opening an IRA account; we're pleased to provide you with this information.
Enclosed please find the documents for signing.	Won't you please sign the papers and return them by Friday?
In checking our records we found that our invoice #3260 is still outstanding.	Have you overlooked paying the bill? If so, please send us your check for $62.40.
On September 4, we sent you some papers for signature. As of this date, no papers have been received.	Did you receive the papers we sent you? Two weeks have passed and we haven't heard from you.

It makes all the difference, doesn't it, when we move away from our old standbys and try some new approaches? So dare to be a little daring—you might like it.

Always keep in mind that our aim in writing is to get our reader involved. One sure-fire way is to include a question in your letter. What happens when I ask you a question? Right! You make a response (even if it's a shrug). Try starting or ending your letter with a question. The following case will give you a good idea of how to use a question to get a result.

Joel sells advertising space for a radio station. Joel had lent a commercial tape to a colleague, who had promised to return the tape right away. Well, Joel tried a variety of tactics—phone calls, letters, more phone calls—and was always told it would be returned shortly. So in his next letter, Joel tried this approach:

Steve, you promised to return the tape of the Three
Star pet food commercial "shortly."
How long is "shortly"?

Guess who got a tape delivered by messenger that day?
That's what I call a letter with results!

Another sure-fire way to get the reader involved is with
a bit of flattery. (Does anyone out there not respond to a
complimentary comment?) So try to include comments such
as these in your letters:

It was a pleasure meeting you today. Thanks,
Woody, for telling me about your department's training needs.

You certainly raised some important issues in your
letter of July 20. I appreciate your bringing them to
my attention, Lynn.

Flattery, or what I prefer to call sincerity, can gain a
rightful place in your arsenal of effective letter openings.

You'll notice, in the previous two examples, the name
of the letter reader was inserted in the body of the letter. Is
this okay? You bet! Don't you like it when someone uses
your name in conversation? Well, why not use names in
your letters as well? And what happens when you hear your
name? Right again—you respond!

The Case for Clear Language

You've mastered the opening and closing statement philosophy. Now what about the stuff that goes in the middle,
the heart of your letter?
Several pointers come to mind:

1. Don't bore your reader with a history first. Or, if you
must, at least make it easy for the reader to know what you

want and to follow the course of events.

2. If you can, make a list of the items to be covered, or of the history—this will make it much easier for the reader to comprehend and will make your letter visually appealing.

3. Remember your purpose for writing, so that all the factual information relates to the purpose.

I can best illustrate these pointers with an honest-to-goodness, word-for-word letter just received by my accountant, Bob Kane. You home owners will love this story.

Here's the background: Bob had made a $1,600 deposit in his checking account to cover his upcoming mortgage payment (this is in California, where housing prices and interest rates are crazy). To Bob's surprise, his mortgage payment check bounced and, to make matters worse, a late payment charge of $83.00 was added on! Bob contacted his bank and learned that the bank had incorrectly read his deposit as $160 instead of $1,600. Bob then asked his bank to write a letter explaining the situation to the mortgage company and requesting that the late payment charge therefore be eliminated.

When Bob related this story, I asked him how he would have worded the letter. Here's his version:

L.K. Mortgage
16640 Ventura Boulevard
Encino, California 91436

> Re: Robert L. Kane
> Acct. No. 1264588

Dear L. K. Mortgage:

Would you please correct an error made by our bank on Mr. Kane's account? Here's what happened:

1. Mr. Kane had deposited a sufficient sum to cover his mortgage payment in his checking account.
2. Our bank credited a lesser sum to his account.

3. Consequently, Mr. Kane's check bounced, and a late charge penalty was assessed against him.

Since Mr. Kane made his payment to you in good faith, we accept responsibility for this unfortunate circumstance and offer our apology. We request that the late penalty charge against his account be waived.

This is the actual letter sent by Bob's bank:

L.K. Mortgage
16640 Ventura Boulevard
Encino, California 91436

Gentlemen:

It has come to our attention that a mutual customer of ours, a one Robert Kane, has incurred a payment penalty through your office due to a returned payment. Mr. Kane has contacted our office to inquire as to the reason for the return and upon close investigation of the matter, we have ascertained that, due to an error in crediting, Mr. Kane's account showed an incorrect balance available.

Since the conclusion of our research into the matter, Mr. Kane's account has been updated to show a corrected balance. Being that Mr. Kane made his payment to you in good faith and under instructions that monies were available in his account, we request that any charges levied against Mr. Kane for non-payment be waived.

We regret any inconvenience this may have caused your office and hope that Mr. Kane's standing with your office will not be adversely affected. If you are in need of further information please feel free to call (213) 588-7933. We appreciate your prompt and courteous consideration of this matter.

There are many things wrong with this letter.

1. What is the purpose of this letter? We start out with ten lines of history before we get to the reason for writing the letter.

2. So many stiff, unnatural phrases:
   - "it has come to our attention"
   - "a mutual customer of ours"
   - "to inquire as to the reason"
   - "we have ascertained"
   - "since the conclusion of our research"
   - "under instructions that monies were available"
   - "any charge levied against"

   I could go on but I'd probably reprint the entire letter.

3. Too much technical jargon:
   - "incurred a payment penalty"
   - "due to a return payment"
   - "incorrect balance available"

4. Lack of an action ending

If you go back to the pointers I raised about writing clearly, you will find that Bob's created version fits the bill; the bank's real letter does not.

One more point and then we'll put this section to bed: Don't write in anger—you won't get results. Instead, your reader will react defensively (and rightfully so: What do *you* do when you're attacked?). What you are interested in, ultimately, is getting results.

So instead of	*Try this*
We just received a late shipment of the wrong merchandise. Didn't you understand my instructions?	We have always received prompt and reliable service from your company. That's why it was such a surprise to receive the wrong merchandise from you and to receive it two weeks late.

In summary then, a letter can confirm, deny, request, inform, promote, remind, suggest, describe, entertain...you name it, a letter can do it!

What do you want your letters to do?

Letter-writing Tips

1. Let your opening and closing statements create favorable impressions for the reader.
2. Ask questions to get the reader involved.
3. Make flattering or sincere comments.
4. Use a person's name in the body of the letter.
5. Don't bore your reader with history.
6. Explain information with lists.
7. Avoid technical terminology.
8. Don't write to complain—write to explain.

Letter Styles/Mechanics

We have concentrated so far on what goes into a letter and how to compose one. What about the mechanics of a letter, how it should look, how it should be arranged on the page, how to proofread?

Yes, those aspects are the responsibility of the person or machine typing your letters, but ultimately, if your signature appears on the letter, the potato is in your lap.

So let's take it from the top...

This is the standard format for setting up a business letter:

1. Most organizations will have their name and address imprinted at the top of their stationery (called letterhead). If you don't have imprinted stationery, then your name and address are placed about two inches down from the top and

about five inches from the left side of the page.

2. Most companies these days favor what is known as the block style for letters: the inside address, date, salutation and closing, and paragraphs all begin at the left margin.

3. The date appears at the left-hand margin, at least three spaces below the company address; then skip two or three spaces and begin the inside address (the reader's address).

4. The inside address appears in this order; an envelope is prepared with this same information:

- reader's name
- reader's title (optional, especially since it takes up line space)
- organization's name
- organization's street address
- city, state, and zip code

5. Many people add an "Attention" line after the inside address, so let me address this situation now. The "Attention" line is reserved for a general address, and is used when a letter is not sent to a specific name. To illustrate, these are *correct*: Attention: Personnel Department; Attention: Accounts Receivable Manager.

The "Attention" line is not to be used when a specific person's name is known. In other words, this is *wrong*: Attention: Mr. Carl Haber. Since you know his name, why not put it at the top of the inside address?

6. A subject line or reference line can appear, usually over toward the right-hand side of the page, to specify such information as:

- account name
- account or invoice number
- date of previous letter
- payment dates and amounts

Actually, you can include any information in the reference line that would otherwise add to the clutter in the letter.

7. The salutation appears two or three spaces below the inside address, like so:

* Dear Mr. Foster:
* Dear John: (use a first name when you know the person and have used his first name)

The person's name in the salutation is followed by a colon (:) because this punctuation mark serves as an introducer for the information that follows.

8. The body of the letter begins two spaces beneath the salutation line, again at the left margin. Skip two spaces between each new paragraph. Don't indent when beginning a new paragraph (unless, of course, that is your company's style).

9. The complimentary closing appears two or three spaces after the final paragraph. Use one of these:

Popular Closings	*Out-of-date Closings*
Sincerely,	Very truly yours,
Cordially,	Yours very truly,
Sincerely yours,	As ever I remain,

10. Your typed name and title (optional) appear three to four spaces beneath the closing.

In between the closing and your typed name, put your signature.

11. References appear two to three spaces below the typed name; these can include:

* Writer's and typist's initials (useful when having to locate who did what) appear as RCS:LW or RCS/LW or rcs:lw. (I think equality has eliminated the old formula of having the typist's initials in small letters and the writer's in capitals.)
* A notation about items included with the letter appears as

"Attachments" or "Enclosures" (usually this word gets a little check mark behind it as the items are sent along with the letter).
- A notation about copies of the letter being sent to other parties appears as "c: Alexander Mills" (the old notation was "cc" but died a quick death when the handy office copier replaced carbon paper).

The skeleton of a business letter looks like this:

Organization name and address

Date

Ms. Alix Foster
GC Premium Company
1043 N. Massachusetts Avenue
Washington, D.C. 20010

Re: Randolph Allison
Acct. No. B. 10654-3

Dear Ms. Foster:

_____
_____
_____

_____
_____
_____

_____
_____
_____
_____

Sincerely,

Anthony B. Morales
Vice-president, Finance

ABM/PN

Attachments

c: Bud Williamson
   Joanne Sellner

But, you may be wondering, if our letters begin with a lot of formality about names, addresses, references and such, how can we get our reader involved right at the beginning? In fact, some inside addresses and reference lines take up so much room that the bodies of our letters don't begin until halfway or more down the page. Is that getting our reader involved—when he or she has to search for the opening of the letter?

A newer, less widely known style takes care of this problem. The format goes like this:

1. Organization letterhead (can't do anything about that because it's imprinted on the paper)
2. The date at the left-hand margin
3. No inside address (at least not at the top of the page)
4. A reference line, if necessary, over toward the right-hand side of the page
5. The salutation line (if you know the reader somewhat personally, you can skip this line and incorporate the reader's name into the body of the letter)
6. The body of the letter
7. The complimentary close
8. Your name and title, and signature in the space between the complimentary closing and your typed name
9. References, if absolutely necessary
10. The reader's address (Let's be logical: the reader is quite familiar with his or her address, so why clutter up the letter with it?)

The skeleton of the modern style of a business letter looks like this:

Organization name and address

Date

Re: Randolph Allison
Acct. No. B 10654–3

Ms. Foster, _____
_____
_____
_____

_____
_____
_____

_____
_____
_____

Sincerely,

Anthony B. Morales
Vice-president, Finance

ABM/PN

Attachments

c: Bud Williamson
   Joanne Sellner

Ms. Alix Foster
GC Premium Company
1043 N. Massachusetts Avenue
Washington, D.C. 20010

Format for Letters

The Standard	*The Latest*
1. Organization letterhead	1. Organization letterhead
2. Date	2. Date
3. Reader's address	3. Reference line
4. Reference line	4. Salutation part of the body of the letter
5. Salutation	5. Body of the letter
6. Body of the letter	6. Closing
7. Closing	7. Signature, typed name and title
8. Signature, typed name and title	8. References
9. References	9. Reader's address

Once you've decided on a format and your letter has been typed, stand back and look at it:

- Does it fill the page—not top-heavy or bottom-heavy?
- Does it look overwhelming with just one or two long paragraphs, or are there a number of separations?
- Is there plenty of free space around the typed words, or does the letter look crowded?
- Are there any mistakes in spelling or punctuation, or any missing words?
- Does it look inviting to read?
- Did you sign the letter?

You answered correctly, you say? You want to send the letter?

In a minute, after you have proofread it, after you've checked the finished letter for any final corrections. You may think that proofreading is not your job; but the letter does carry your signature, so who's in charge?

> ## *Proofreading Tips*
>
> 1. Check all spelling and punctuation.
> 2. Verify all figures and dates for accuracy.
> 3. Use a ruler to help you read one line at a time.
> 4. Read the letter aloud to yourself or, preferably, to another person.

Everything okay? Now you can send that great letter. But remember... Write to explain, entertain, retain, and gain—but not to complain.

And do it again!

Memos

The interoffice memorandum, or memo, is commonly used for exchanging information among people in the same organization. The memo gives us a permanent record of general news, a particular course of action, an identified problem, a project's progress—in short, any information relating to the successful carrying on of a business.

The memo has a number of advantages:

- It can be sent to multiple people in the organization, thus keeping everyone simultaneously informed.
- It can save time for those who get their information from memos and then make decisions based on what they've read.
- It gives the writer practice in thinking clearly and presenting information logically.
- It serves as a written record of a course of action.
- It carries that special impact of putting events in writing.

The memo has a few disadvantages as well:

- It takes longer to compose and transmit than a phone call.
- It can get tied up in the interoffice mail or in someone's "in" box.
- The writer doesn't usually get an immediate reply to the memo; and sometimes there's no feedback at all.

But the advantages of writing a memo outweigh the disadvantages, especially when you want to make a positive, lasting impression, and in this section we'll examine the means for writing effective memos.

Objectives of a Memo

Keep in mind that in many organizations the memo is relied upon as a major source of information for management. This is not a judgment—how else can many people simultaneously be kept aware of events and changes? And in these times of varying work schedules, business trips, and heavy workload commitments, the memo may be the best and only means for keeping that awareness at an active and safe level.

Memos, therefore, should meet these criteria:

1. Serve as a vehicle for exchanging thoughts or presenting information
2. Present information in a clear and concise fashion
3. Present information in a short and readable form
4. Document or recommend a particular course of action
5. Anticipate and address the reader's questions or objections

How to Write a Memo that Gets Read

The word *memo* is short for memorandum, but these days memos are anything but short. Pull out a few from your files, any will do. How many pages are they? One I hope, but more likely two or three or four (don't tell me about more).

Memos should be short, a page or two at the most; otherwise they won't get carefully read. (Remember our finding about letters?: Correspondence of more than one page puts the reader off.) Think of your audience's reading time. Your memo is probably just one of many received that day, so what are your chances of getting read if your memo is wordy and long?

Sure, I know, your boss has to read this memo—she requested it. But will she read it with interest, or will she skim over the three pages trying to find the important facts? How can you write a memo so that it will be read?

The process of writing a memo is very similar to the process of writing a business letter. Memos are sometimes easier to write because you usually know your readers through your working relationship and therefore have a clearer idea of the kind of information they need and like.

The most important thing to keep in mind about memo writing is this: Your reader may not have much time to read your memo, so make your reader's time worthwhile.

And with the reader in mind, let's begin to construct a memo. Where do we start? With the purpose for writing, of course.

How to Organize A Memo

1. Identify your purpose by asking yourself "Why am I writing?"
2. Write your purpose on a piece of paper or an index card—or on your CRT screen if you're in an "office of the future."
3. Compose a list of the information you want to cover in the memo; write ideas down as you think of them—don't be concerned just yet about the order.
4. Reread your list of facts and see if any ideas belong with others; group those together.

5. Think categories. Arrange your ideas under head-
   ings; for example:
   • Statement of the problem
   • Recommendations
   • Product development
   • Advantages and disadvantages
   • Department plan
   • Changes for staff personnel

   Think of your headings as road signs; your reader
   will be helped by knowing what section is coming up.
   And thinking in categories will automatically get you
   on the organized path.
6. Arrange your categories in logical sequence.
7. Arrange your facts within each category in logical
   sequence, always keeping in mind your purpose
   for writing.
8. Decide on an ending action; this could take the
   form of a request to get together, a call for a decision, a statement about what to do with the
   memo—whatever it is that you or the reader should
   do next.

So you understand the process of getting organized. You
say your trouble is the words to use, not the framework.
Well, you are not alone.

I recently read about the head of a governmental agency
who has gone on a campaign to straighten out his department's language by getting rid of vague wordings and con-
voluted phrases. In fact, the word processing machine in
the department has been programmed to come to a stop
when one of the no-no words is entered.

This might seem a little drastic to us, but I can appreciate
the reasoning. It's taught in writing classes as the KISS
concept—*Keep it simple, stupid*: If we cut out all the unnecessary garbage, the writer has less to write, the typist

less to type, and the reader less to read. All quite commendable, but let me give you my own feelings.

I will never, abolutely never, tell you to not use a particular word or phrase. Sure, I can tell you not to use the expression "Enclosed please find" because it sounds as if you're literally asking the reader to search for something, and I can tell you to substitute "Here is [whatever]" for it. But suppose you find yourself getting just as tired of saying "Here is" as you were about "Enclosed please find"? And what if one day you find yourself writing "I am enclosing"?

Here's where I think I can give you my best advice: Be aware of alternatives; look for options; but above all, always remember your own sanity . . . and your reader's. There are times when you will want to say, "I would like to express my appreciation," even though "Thank you" is five words shorter. As the writer, you deserve a break from time to time. Vary your expressions. But *always* be aware of your reader's expectations and level of understanding. . . . Dress to fit in at the party.

How to Write a Memo with Punch

An effective memo is one that gets results. And to get results we must use words that are clear, complete, concise, and correct.

There are three other concepts to consider in writing an effective memo: We must try to be creative, credible, and considerate.

These ingredients all add up to the seven C's of effective writing:

The Seven C's of Effective Writing

1. Be Clear   Have a definite purpose for writing
                               and state that purpose in the "Subject" line of the memo; use a very
                               specific title. Repeat the purpose
                               in the beginning of the memo. Use

words that your reader can understand. Organize your thoughts around your purpose in a logical sequence. Use specific direct words instead of vague ones.

Unclear Subject: Disaster Plan
Clear Subject: Recommendation to Revise the Companywide Disaster Plan

Unclear Purpose: Our department has encountered numerous problems with shipments over the past two months. For example . . .

Clear Purpose: Our department has had shipment problems since December, and I'd like to offer some solutions:

Vague Words: The implementation of the new plan will commence within two or three weeks.

Direct Words: The new plan will begin around April 15th.

2. Be Complete

Include all necessary facts and background information. The facts mentioned should support the purpose for writing, and should be reliable and timely.

Try to anticipate questions that the reader might have or ask. Be aware of how familiar your reader is with the subject. Provide as much information as is needed for your reader to understand and evaluate your memo.

Incomplete Facts: This study revealed that a great number of hospitals in the city have emergency care facilities.

Complete Facts:	We studied 120 hospitals in the city and found that 85 of them (70%) have emergency care facilities.

3. Be Concise

Make the reader understand the information—as quickly and as easily as possible. Always keep in mind the reader's knowledge of the subject and the reader's time constraints. Remember, the most read memos are the shortest and clearest ones.

Reread every point in your memo and ask yourself, "Does this need to be included?"

Be careful about taking out too much, though. You don't want to risk eliminating important facts just for the sake of being brief.

Things to avoid:
- repetition and padding
- wordiness
- unnecessary details
- long complex sentences

Things to include:
- precise phrases
- relevant details
- short words and short sentences
- brief thoughts

Not Concise:	As evidenced by the previously furnished data, we have every reason to conclude that the proposed project is not a viable one.
Concise:	Our data show that we should not proceed with this project.

4. Be Correct	Check that all information is accurate, especially figures and dates. Make sure that all spelling, grammar, and punctuation is correct—proofread your memo.
5. Be Credible	Strive for believability in your writing. Present yourself as a reliable and competent person. After all, that is why you're writing, isn't it?
6. Be Creative	Think about some alternative ways for presenting the information. Get away from the straight narrative, reading from left to right approach:

- Can the information be presented in a question and answer format?
- Think graphics—use tables and charts to show comparisons
- Make lists of ideas
- Make it easy for your reader to respond.

Dull: In March we sold 600 packages of paper clips; in April and May we sold 750 packages, a 25% increase, and in June we sold 1,000.

Creative: Our sales of paper clips for the past quarter are:

Month	Packages Sold
March	600
April	750
May	750
June	1,000

Dull:

Please let me know what color paper you prefer for your new stationery. I've attached samples of the various shades of blue.

Creative:

Here are the samples of the different colors of paper for your new stationery. Please mark your choice and return this memo to me. I'll place your order as soon as I hear from you.

___ I like medium blue

___ I like pale blue

___ I like sky blue

_____

Signature

7. Be considerate

Think of your reader: Make it worthwhile for your reader to spend time on your memo. Make sure your memo sounds as if it was written by one human being for another. Try to let some of your personality come through. Ask yourself, "Why should my reader spend time reading this? How can I get my reader involved?"

Cold:

Sales projections for the next twelve months are itemized below.

Caring:

These sales projections for the next twelve months should help your department to develop upcoming staffing schedules.

Components of a Well-Written Memo

1. Purpose stated early in the memo:
   - The purpose should be clearly mentioned in the first paragraph.
   - The purpose doesn't always have to be the first sentence, but it should be close.

2. Purpose stated clearly in the memo:
   - Have a simple and direct statement to explain why the memo has been written.
   - State the benefit to the reader.

3. Direct, to the point statements:
   - The words should be relevant.
   - The ideas presented should support the basic purpose of the memo: either passing along information or presenting recommendations.

4. Well-organized writing:
   - The words should flow from idea to idea and sentence to sentence.
   - The ideas should be cohesive and make sense to the reader.

5. Easy to read format:
   - Does the memo have a specific title and headings? Let the reader know what the subject is and where the sections separate.
   - Is the material interesting? Can it be told through graphs or charts?
   - Is the language understandable to the reader?
   - Is the wording informal? Does it require translation?
   - Is the memo brief? Does it contain short words and sentences?

- Does some of the writer's personality show through?
- Does the memo look attractive? Is there lots of white space, wide margins, paragraphs?

Memo Styles/Mechanics

What does a memo look like? What's the difference between the format of a memo and a letter? Interoffice memos are more informal than letters: No inside address is needed, no salutation line, no complimentary close, and no signature.

1. Usually the organizations's name appears at the top, followed by one of these phrases:

- Interoffice memorandum
- Interoffice communication
- Internal correspondence
- Memorandum

or another similar variation.

2. The memo usually has some preprinted headings a few spaces below the name, and these include:

To:	Date:
From:	Copies to:
Subject:	

These headings may run vertically down the left side of the page, or they may be separated into columns (as in the above example); either way is correct and, of course, is a matter of company style.

And some companies use the word *Re* (regarding) instead of *Subject*.

The information in the headings would be:

To: the name of the person or department receiving the memo; for example:

To: Albert Remsen, Office Manager
To: All Regional Vice-presidents
To: Finance Department Staff

From: the name of the person or department issuing
           the memo; for example:
           From: Cynthia Smythe, Regional Coordinator
           From: Policy and Procedures Committee
           From: Steve Grayson and Rebecca Gaylord,
                 Planning Division

Date: the date the memo is issued

Subject: a clear statement about the topic treated in the
           memo; for example:
           Subject: Changes in Reporting Hours
           Re: Increased Employee Benefits
           Re: Recommendation to Stagger Lunch
                     Hours

Copies to: the names of other individuals, in addition to
           the main reader, who need to be informed about
           this subject; usually these names are listed in
           order of company position or protocol; when in
           doubt, it's always safe to list names alphabeti-
           cally:

                    James B. Hall, Divisional
                       Vice-president
                    Rona L. Tyson, Vice-president
                    Charles Nelson, Vice-president
                    Tom Whittaker, Assistant
                       Vice-president
                                    or

                    James B. Hall
                    Charles Nelson
                    Rona L. Tyson
                    Tom Whittaker

3. The body of the memo begins a few spaces below the memo headings, at the left margin. Skip two spaces between each new paragraph.

4. Instead of a signature, put your initials next to your name in the "From" line. You can, if it is company policy, sign the memo, but all that is actually required is a set of initials.

The skeleton of a memo looks like this:

Organization Name
Inter-Office Correspondence

To:	Phyllis White	**Date:**	February 15, 1982
	Director, Purchasing		
From:	Scott Gross,	**Copies to:**	All Purchasing
	Purchasing Agent		Agents
Re:	Request to Change Office Supplies Vendor		

_____
_____
_____
_____

How to Avoid Being Buried under Memos

As you're reading this section, you might be saying to yourself, "So far I've learned how to recognize and write effective memos. But it sounds as if I'm going to be spending a lot of time writing and reading memos. Is that so?"

Let me offer some guidelines about when to write and when not to write a memo:

Don't Write	*Do Write*
If the situation can be settled in person or on the telephone	If you want to follow up on the meeting or conversation with a written reinforcement

Don't Write	*Do Write*
If the situation has emotional overtones to it; think through the issue before writing about it—or, better yet, talk to the involved parties	If the situation is noncontroversial and won't backfire in your face
To show off or brag about your latest accomplishment	To inform concerned parties about your achievements—especially if they affect these parties

Who gets copies of the memo? My advice is to make doubly sure that everyone on your distribution list really needs to be informed about the contents of your memo. Avoid sending people copies of your memos to call attention to your latest achievement. Distribute copies only to those people who are directly concerned with the issues raised in your memo. When in doubt, share your proposed distribution list with your boss or an alert colleague. Keep in mind that your reader may not have much time to read your memo; value your reader's time.

It isn't enough to know *how* to write a memo—we also have to assess *when* to write a memo. And who said writing was simple? Actually, writing *is* simple; it's all the thought before and during the process that is so troublesome. Therefore, keep these thoughts in mind:

1. Write to bring the news up to date.
2. Tell your audience the necessary news.
3. Present the information in a short, direct form.
4. Be prepared and organized.
5. Present information in a form that can be passed along as is to others.
6. Discuss relevant achievements.
7. Make the audience's reading time worthwhile.

8. Keep your audience continuously aware of events—
   not just at crisis times.
9. Project a human approach.
10. Keep the audience's interest.
11. Keep communication lines open.
12. Let your writing show your competency.

Reports

When to Write a Report versus a Memo

"Write me a memo"...sounds easy, doesn't it? "Send me a report"...now that sounds ominous. Don't be scared off by the sound of it, though—a report is just a fleshed-out memo. A report has more sections or parts to it than a memo has, so consequently it seems a bit more formal. But the development, writing, and organization of a report follow the same principles and techniques you have already mastered in learning how to write effective memos. So writing a report should be a snap for you—it will just take a little more time.

How to decide between preparing a report or a memo? Ask yourself two questions:

1. Will the information fill more than two pages?
2. Do I want to make a special impact?

If you have two yes votes, then a report is the way to go. The report is the most authoritative and professional document you can prepare; you'll be proud to submit a report to management.

All business reports have the same purpose: to convey information to those who need it; sometimes to help in making decisions, but always to keep interested parties aware of events that are taking place.

Reports fall into three categories:

Information reports: These reports present data and state what happened during the course of an event or a project.

Recommendation reports: These reports also present data, but go beyond that to propose action to take or a procedure to follow.

Periodic or progress reports: These reports present a record of activities, usually charted by weeks or months, and explain what was completed and what remains to be completed.

Reports are designed to meet these objectives:

- To give management a capsulized explanation of a problem area or a plan of study
- To transmit factual information for use in future planning or decision making
- To present useful information in a readable form
- Sometimes to recommend a course of action

Information and recommendation reports are developed and organized in a similar fashion. Progress reports are a bit different, and tips for writing them will be covered in a separate section.

First, let's take a look at information and recommendation reports.

Format for Information and Recommendation Reports

A report can be divided into three major sections—introductory material, body material, and supplementary material—with each section having distinct and necessary parts:

The *introductory material* comprises these parts:

a. Cover memo or letter of transmittal
  - used when the report will be distributed to multiple readers
  - explains the purpose, scope, and time span of the report
  - tells the success of the study, problems encountered, personal benefits gained, and any budget or time limitations; in short, any information not related to the factual data presented within the report

b. Title page
  - the title of the report usually appears in the center of the page
  - other information to appear on the title page:
    —author's name
    —date prepared
    —name of the department, individual, or organization requesting the report

c. Report summary or synopsis
  - the report summary is written *after* the report is completed, but it appears at the front of the report
  - the reader looks to the summary for an idea of what the report is all about
  - summarizes the core information presented in the report, including recommendations, if any
  - the summary is a mini-report, highlighting the entire report for the reader
  - the summary should be no longer than one or two pages
  - the summary is placed at the beginning of the report, since the reader is most interested in the conclusions and recommendations presented

d. Table of Contents
  - presents the reader with a handy reference tool

- lists all of the report sections or headings and their page numbers
- lists charts and graphs included in each section

The *body material* comprises these parts:

a. Statement of the report's purpose
   - presents a clear explanation and overview of what was to be accomplished
   - gives the "who, what, where, when, and why" of what was to be accomplished

b. Recommendations (if any)
   - recommendations are placed at the very *beginning* of the report for the reader's ease in learning what further actions should be taken
   - the recommendations section presents a detailed description of how specific recommendations can be effectively carried out
   - you must have a workable plan; it isn't enough to state what should be done—you need to state how it can be done
   - cite a recommendation for each identified problem

c. Findings and Methodology
   - contains the scope and analysis of what you set out to do
   - shows how you accomplished what you set out to do
   - serves as backup justification for your recommendations, since this section specifies how the conclusions and recommendations were reached

d. Conclusions
   - presents the final solutions, based on the evidence found during the course of the study
   - explains how all conclusions were reached, as a result of the study.

The *supplementary material* comprises these parts:

a. Appendix
   • lists any tables, explanations of terms, graphs, and exhibits that were not placed in the body of the report
b. Bibliography
   • lists sources of information, such as books or articles.

Those are the parts of a report, but you're probably still in the same bind: How to write a good one?

How to Prepare a Report

Your first step in preparing a report is to define exactly what is wanted from the report: Who will read it? How will it be used? What function will it serve?

Next, figure out how you will gather the information for your report: Is it all in your head? Will you take notes? Do you need to do some research (at the library or by reading other reports on the subject)? Do you need to talk to other people?

Third, prepare a preliminary outline, but try this new method for organizing. If you know how to play rummy, this will be easy and fun:

1. Get a stack of index cards.
2. Think of the points you want to make in the report and write each point on a card—only one point per card.
3. Hold the cards in your hand and look for the ones that are related to one another.
4. Shuffle the cards as many times as you like in order to see different possibilities and relationships among the various points.
5. Think categories: Make title or heading cards for your groups of related points.
6. Arrange your categories and cards in sequential order: Which information should be presented first? Which in-

formation must appear before others in order to make
the others clear?

Now you should have an organized body of information.
The index card method greatly simplifies report writing; it
helps you organize logically, by not being confined to any
written order of words. And once you have your headings
and points in order, the groundwork for your report has been
completed.

Here's how the index card system was used in an actual
situation:

Christopher Portugal, a department manager, wants to
make a recommendation to his boss, the division manager,
to develop a system for keeping track of all the training
classes and seminars his staff members attend. Right now,
this information is kept in an informal and haphazard fashion.

Christopher talks to other department managers to find
out how they handle the situation and also consults with his
contacts at other companies. After thinking through his plan
Christopher makes these notes, each one on a separate index
card. (I've numbered them here so that it will be easier to
arrange them in categories without having to repeat myself,
but you wouldn't necessarily have to number your ideas.)
Remember, you don't have to have complete thoughts—
just enough to help you identify major information to cover:

1. Recommend we develop formal tracking system for
   training
2. No system now; everyone independent
3. Want to encourage people to go to seminars to improve
4. Need forms to complete
5. Training coordinator to handle duties
6. Could be more cost-effective to get group rates if we
   knew needs in advance

7. Don't have way of identifying and providing training needs
8. Four needs to be satisfied
9. Write procedures to be followed
10. How to coordinate training requests
11. Who completes and signs forms
12. Limits on how many classes to take and where
13. No way to link performance appraisals with educational needs
14. Need to have central point for collecting data
15. Too many sources for training
16. Develop policy for maintaining skills
17. Need to develop training plans
18. Role of training coordinator

Christopher figures that should about do it for notes. Now he groups the related ideas together in these configurations:

> 1
> 2, 6, 7, 13, 14, 15
> 3, 8, 16
> 10, 11, 12, 17, 18
> 4
> 9
> 5

Now he gives these points category headings:

> Recommendation—1
> Background—2, 6, 7, 13, 14, 15
> Policy statement—3, 8, 16
> Guidelines—10, 11, 12, 17, 18
> Forms—4
> Procedures—9
> Action Plan—5

And then he arranges his categories and points in sequential order:

> Recommendation—1
> Background—2, 14, 7, 13, 6, 15
> Policy statement—3, 16, 8
> Guidelines—10, 18, 11, 17, 12
> Forms—4
> Procedures—9
> Action Plan—5

The information for Christopher's report is now organized, and it didn't take very long. He is ready to write his recommendation report. Working with his index cards he fleshes out the major ideas and adds a few minor ones. The writing is easier to tackle now because Christopher has such a good idea of what he wants to say.

After writing the proposal, Christopher adds a title page and a cover memo—and the report will soon be on its way to his readers. The finished product appears on the following pages.

Interoffice Memo

To: Grant Cunningham   *Date:*   February 10, 1982
           Division Manager

From: Christopher Portugal   *Copy to:* Pat Wilhite
           Department Manager   Personnel Director

Subject: A Proposal to Provide a Formal Training and
           Tracking System at LPP

We do not have a formal system for providing training programs to our employees, nor do we have a system for keeping track of who attends seminars. I would like to recommend that LPP develop such a formalized system.

Proposal

The attached document represents the proposed program for a systematized approach to provide training and tracking for the growth of personnel. The document is broken down into the following sections:

> Recommendation
> Background
> Policy statement
> Guidelines
> Forms
> Procedures
> Action Plan

Let's get together at your earliest convenience to discuss my proposal. I really feel the need to develop a more systematic approach to training than what we are currently providing.

A Proposal to Provide a Formal Training and Tracking System at LPP

Prepared for: Grant Cunningham,
Division Manager

Prepared by: Christopher Portugal,
Department Manager

February 10, 1982

A Proposal to Provide a Formal Training and Tracking System at LPP

Recommendation

I would like to recommend that LPP develop a formalized program for providing and keeping track of the various training seminars and workshops attended by all LPP personnel.

Background

- There is no formalized system in place for the selection of candidates or courses to be attended.
- Every LPP division currently manages training independently.
- There is no central point for the control or the collection of background data.
- Current methods are not cost-effective, as they do not provide for group rates or in-house training.
- Employees are being sent to similar courses through different sources.
- Current methods do not provide for a link between the employee's performance appraisal and the educational needs identified through this process.
- Current methods take a haphazard approach to training plans, resulting in a reactive mode of management.

Proposed Policy Statement

LPP encourages its employees to attend workshops and seminars related to maintaining professional skills and expanding their career growth.

All training will be done to satisfy four basic needs:

1. Organizational career planning needs as a result of promotions or transfers.
2. Management/technical needs due to evaluated deficiencies.

3. Technical needs due to changes in technologies (e.g., new operating systems, new equipment or methodologies, and new software packages).
4. Individual needs for growth.

Proposed Guidelines

The following guidelines will apply:

1. All training requests will require coordination with the personnel training coordinator and approval by the appropriate departmental or division manager.
2. Training evaluation forms must be completed for all individuals selected for training.
3. Training plans should be developed from the evaluation forms.
4. Training plans must be specific as to the needs of the individual and, where possible, establish the relationship between the request and the employee's performance appraisal.
5. Training plans and training selection will be the responsibility of the immediate manager and will be coordinated with the personnel training coordinator. The coordinator will suggest courses, based on those already taken by other employees.
6. A total of three weeks per year per individual in seminars/workshops/tutorships/conferences, etc., will be granted for training purposes.
7. Where possible, the geographical selection for courses must be given in this order: (1) Los Angeles, (2) within California, and (3) out of state.

Proposed Forms

The following forms will be utilized in making the plans:

1. Training evaluation form
2. Training plan
3. Enrollment request

In addition, the following information will be available from the coordinator:

1. Training data base (information on available courses)
2. Course evaluation data base (input on courses taken)

Proposed Procedures

Manager

1. Complete evaluation of selected employee or manager, applying the set of guidelines outlined in the policy statement.
2. Review evaluation form with appropriate superior and gain approval.
3. Review available classes/seminars/conferences with the personnel training coordinator.
4. Prepare enrollment request and forward with evaluation form to immediate superior for review and approval.

Personnel
Training
Coordinator

1. Review enrollment request.
2. Verify approval signatures.
3. Verify class/seminar availability.
4. Make necessary arrangements for reservations and billing.
5. Forward a copy to department secretary for travel and accommodation arrangements.
6. Notify submitting manager of decision.
7. Forward a copy to Finance and Accounting for accounting purposes.
8. Update training data base for courses taken.
9. Provide printouts of these data bases to executive committee.
10. Prepare quarterly class/seminar report for executive committee.

Action Plan

The training department is prepared to take on the responsibility of coordinating and keeping track of all companywide training plans. This responsibility will be handled by the present training coordinator.

The systems and procedures outlined in this proposal have been reviewed by and are acceptable to the training department. As soon as this proposal has been modified, if necessary, and approved by the division management, training will proceed to put the procedures into effect.

How to Edit a Report

Editing is not rewriting; the first draft should be the one you edit into a finished product. And editing is not just the process of rereading your report to cut out unnecessary words. Instead you want to examine the report with a fresh eye, with the reader's eye. So the key to editing a report is to look at it from the reader's point of view.

When you're editing, concentrate on what is said. Examine the words you're using. Do your words show who has the responsibility for the actions? The way to show responsibility is by using the "active voice" rather than the "passive voice." Let me illustrate this point:

Common expressions found in reports are "It was determined" or "A suggestion was made" or "It is recommended." Instead say, "We found that" and "Jim Brown suggested" and "I recommend." That's taking responsibility. Of course, you will find yourself at times wanting to avoid taking responsibility; that's okay, as long as you are aware of your reasons and don't just fall into the habit of using the passive voice in writing.

Here are some tips explaining how to take yourself through the editing process.

How to Edit

1. Let some time pass between the writing and the editing stages:
   - The ideal method is to write one day and review the next; at the very least, let a few hours pass.

2. Read your opening statements:
   • Do you tell the reader what the subject is?
   • Is the intent of the report clear?

3. Review your recommendations, if any:
   • Do they sound logical?
   • Do they appear to be workable?

4. Read the report from the reader's point of view:
   • Do you have questions about some of the information?
   • Can you identify the people mentioned and terms used in the report?
   • Is the information presented relevant to the original purpose of the report?
   • Do the ideas flow smoothly from one sentence to the next and from one paragraph to the next?
   • Is any information missing?
   • Do the conclusions seem logical?

5. Revise your words so they sound right:
   • Clear up any unclear words or phrases.
   • Check your grammar.
   • Cut out extra words.
   • Eliminate repetitions.
   • Change weak words to strong ones: Use active voice words to make your writing stronger.

Where to Put Charts and Graphs

Visual aids such as charts, graphs, and exhibits can clarify your report. They strengthen ideas and help the reader "see" your point.

The big question about visual aids is where to put them—right after the point, before it, or at the back of the report? Try this technique: If your visual aids are easy to understand and relevant to your point, place them in the body of the report—right after their mention or description. If they are complex or not essential to your point, place them in the appendix as supplementary material. Otherwise an unnecessary or complex chart will only slow or confuse the reader.

Here is an example of a visual aid:

Appendix C
Age Distribution of Automobile Shops

(for period ending 11/30/79)

Name	Month Established	Age (in months)	Total Capital*
Crescent Hill Motor Works	November 1976	37	$74,298
Precision Motor Works	November 1977	25	57,925
Auto-Mechanical	June 1979	6	48,076
West Bay	August 1979	4	36,283
L & M	September 1979	3	20,000
Mid-City Motor Works	November 1979	1	27,989

A full listing of all charts and exhibits in the report should be listed in the table of contents of the report. Be sure to list the page numbers for each exhibit.

The advantages of using visual aids are many:

1. They help the reader find specific items of interest.
2. Material can be presented in a more concise form than is possible any other way.

*Equity and Loans

3. Discussion of material is simplified in chart form.
4. The reader is able to see cause and effect of ideas.
5. The reader is able to see relationships between ideas, especially with statistics.
6. Information is easily grasped and quickly transmitted.
7. The reader's interest is heightened when looking at a chart or table.

And keep in mind these pointers when you are working with visual aids:

1. Visual aids should be simple, not overburdened with too many facts and numbers.
2. Use clear titles and column headings.
3. Visual aids are just that—they are not substitutes for textual explanations; make sure your explanation is clear and then supplement it with a chart.

A final reminder about preparing a report: Give yourself plenty of time to organize it, write it, and review it.

Effective Report Writing

1. Group your ideas into categories—look for an order.
2. Begin with a statement of your purpose—not a history of past events.
3. Set off ideas with headings and indentations so that your reader knows what to expect in the upcoming section.
4. Make lists of ideas and introduce them as lists.
5. Use figures, dollar amounts, and percentages to show relationships—in place of narrative.
6. Avoid big words when smaller ones will do and usually are easier to understand.

7. Use charts and graphs as explanations, not as substitutions.
8. Try for some personality in your writing—use personal names; let your human side show through your writing.
9. Take responsibility for your findings—use the active voice in constructing sentences.
10. End with an action item—state what you want the reader to do or how the plan will be carried out.

Why Write Progress Reports?

- Do you want to keep track of the projects you're working on?
- Do you want to have a record of your successes and setbacks?
- Do you want to keep your boss or others informed of your activities?
- Do you want to have a method for helping you follow up on work in progress?
- Do you want to know where your time goes?
- Do you want to get a raise?

Gotcha! I knew I would on the last question. Progress reports won't guarantee your getting a raise, but they can help you and others stay aware of your regular activities, new or proposed projects, problems encountered, progress made, revised schedules—in short, anything that might help or hinder your success.

Some of you may already be writing progess reports; if not, you should. It's a marvelous way to maintain your visibility in the organization: If you write one for the month of December and then follow up with one for January, by February your boss will be looking forward to receiving it.

A monthly progress report benefits everyone: A progress report lets you know whether your work is on target. If you said originally you would finish your project by April and it's now mid-March and nowhere near completion, well what happened? Why aren't you finished? With monthly project reports you would have documented evidence to explain why the project went wrong or what other events came into play that kept you from sticking to the original schedule. And your boss would also have that evidence and might not have to jump down your throat.

A progress report can help you and others see what you're doing now and compare it to what you did last month, three months ago, eight months ago, last year, and so on. It's a wonderful technique for keeping you and others very aware of your actions. Send it to your boss; send it to key people in your department. Make your own people write progress reports to submit to you—that's a great way to keep up your own awareness level of what's going on in your department. Chart your own progress and look at it objectively. Look at your activities and gauge which things aren't proceeding too well; then you'll know what you need to change, to add to, or to do to get back on the track.

Does it sound as if I'm high on progress reports? I am! I'm self-employed and no one sees my progress reports, but I still write one every month—a fifteen-year habit is tough to break. The report helps me to focus in on my strong and weak areas and to stir my sagging memory about activities needing follow-up.

A progress report also helps me know how my time is being spent. I need to know this so I can measure my activities and assess which ones are "profitable" for me—which activities are worth pursuing in terms of my time and energy and which should probably be written off because I'm not getting reasonable results. I can see what I'm doing now and compare that to my activities of last month or last year. The progress reports help me keep track of a variety of clients and activities so I can follow up on them.

A monthly progress report will help you keep track of everything you do and where your time is spent each month. If your days are anything like mine, you probably start off with a good plan and before you know it it's 3:00 P.M. and you don't know where the day went. Progress reports will help you see that you are actually accomplishing more things than you realize.

If you prepare a progress report each month, at the end of the year you'll have twelve reports that will attest to your accomplishments. And that's how progress reports can help you get a raise: When it's time for your annual review you can go to your boss and say, "This is what I accomplished this year; these are the improvements I've made, these are the ways I have proved our department's credibility. Therefore, that is why I deserve a salary adjustment."

What most of us do instead is to wait until performance evaluation time rolls around and then try to complete our appraisal forms. We sit there and scratch our heads and ask, "What did I accomplish this year? What can I say about my performance?" It's tough to remember what we do from week to week and month to month. But when you have twelve reports representing a year's accomplishments, charting how you achieved your goals and objectives, you will have all the information needed for making an honest self-assessment and completing your performance evaluation.

And if you write progress reports regularly, you'll gain another benefit — information you can keep adding to your résumé. A résumé should not be something you put together when you decide it's time to look for a job; it's a tool for self-assessment, for recording your achievements, for weighing your success in meeting your goals. It should show how valuable a person you are — and you can develop your résumé with the help of your progress reports.

Are you convinced yet about the value of progress reports? Good! Now on to how to write one.

How to Write Progress Reports

Start by keeping simple records of how your day is spent. Many people use their desk or pocket calendars to keep track of time. Or you can try this approach:

1. Take a piece of paper and put the date at the top; or enter the date in your video terminal:
   - Tuesday, February 16, 1982
   - Week of February 15–19, 1982

2. Make some categories for yourself, according to your usual activities. Some sample categories might be:
   - Meetings
   - Telephone calls
   - Reports and memos
   - Employee relations

Or you might organize your categories according to the various functions of your job:
   - Space allocation project
   - Promotional design work
   - Employee meetings
   - Business development
   - Training program
   - Computer assistance

3. List your categories, leaving room between each category so you can plug in the information.
4. As you work on a project, make some notes describing your activities. You can include what you did, any problems encountered, responsible parties, decisions made, and other related information.

5. Keep adding to your notes, and adding categories as you take on new projects and complete old ones.
6. At the end of the month, prepare a progress report using your standard categories. Summarize the pertinent information (you don't have to include every phone call you made, just the ones that affect your continuing projects) within each category, making sure to include progress, setbacks, changes, good news, decisions made, future plans, and an overall appraisal of the progress so far.

My general advice in writing progress reports is to think in categories rather than by dates. You and your reader will have a better grasp of the importance of your activities if you group them in some logical categorical order instead of in chronological order.

Here's an example of what I mean. This progress report is arranged in date format.

Progress Report by Dates

To:	Rex Kennedy	*Date:*	January 2, 1982
	Vice-president		
From:	Lynn Pierson	*Re:*	Progress Report for
	Manager, Word		December 1981
	Processing Center		

December was a short work month because of the holiday festivities and the company-granted vacation during Christmas week, but nevertheless we did manage to accomplish much toward getting people familiar with our new Word Processing Center. To summarize the month's activities for you:

On December 2, a meeting was held to introduce senior management of the real estate division to the new Word Processing Center. They are eager to begin using the center and will send samples of their usual work to me early in

January. I expect to have them trained and using our services by mid-January.

On December 5, I spent the afternoon at our branch office in Burbank as the guest of Louise Smythe, manager of the center. I thought it would be worthwhile to familiarize myself with their systems and procedures, and I came back with a number of good ideas. (I'll report on them as they are implemented.)

Darlene Torres was hired on December 9. She is presently a temporary correspondence secretary on the night shift. She will become a permanent secretary in February and transfer to the day shift, where we have a greater need.

I recently celebrated my five-year anniversary with the company and enjoyed a pleasant lunch with Bob Anderson, director of personnel.

Three pieces of equipment were delivered and installed on the twelfth. Three of our operators, Connie Thompson, Craig Newman, and Joan Kardis, have been trained to use the machines. So far they have had only positive things to say about the equipment.

The logistics department is satisfied with the quality of our work and has requested us to take on more transcription work. (They are pleased with our reduced turnaround time from two days to one.) On December 14, I met with key members of the department to discuss their needs and to examine the types of work they would like us to take on.

Various examples of the kinds of work produced by the accounting department were submitted early in the month, and we began to process their work in the center on December 16. The staff members are pleased with our one-day turnaround time.

Just before the holidays, two permanent correspondence secretarial positions were filled; we still have one vacant position. Our staff as of the end of 1981 numbers five permanent and three temporary correspondence secretaries.

*   *   *

In this form of progress report, where information is arranged by dates, everything is equal. We can't really grasp just how much progress was made because there's no shape or order to the information; everything carries equal weight.

Now compare the chronological format with the category format, using exactly the same information:

Progress Report by Categories

To:	Rex Kennedy Vice-president	*Date:*	January 2, 1982
From:	Lynn Pierson Manager, Word Processing Center	*Re:*	Progress Report for December 1981

December was a short work month because of the holiday festivities and the company-granted vacation during Christmas week, but nevertheless we did manage to accomplish much toward getting people familiar with our new Word Processing Center. To summarize the month's activities for you:

New User Departments

Real Estate

On December 2, a meeting was held to introduce senior management of the real estate division to the new Word Processing Center. They are eager to begin using the center and will send samples of their usual work to me early in January. I expect to have them trained and using our services by mid-January.

Accounting

Various examples of the kinds of work produced by the accounting department were submitted early in the month, and we began to process their work in the center on December 16. The staff members are pleased with our one-day turnaround time.

Continuing User Departments

Logistics

The logistics department is satisfied with the quality of our work and has requested us to take on more transcription work. (They are pleased with our reduced turnaround time from two days to one day.) On December 14 I met with key members of the department to discuss their needs and to examine the types of work they would like us to take on.

Equipment

Three pieces of equipment were delivered and installed on the twelfth. Three of our operators, Connie Thompson, Craig Newman, and Joan Kardis, have been trained to use the machines. So far they have had only positive things to say about the equipment.

Department Staffing

Darlene Torres was hired on December 9. She is presently a temporary correspondence secretary on the night shift. She will become a permanent secretary in February and transfer to the day shift, where we have a greater need.

Just before the holidays, two permanent correspondence secretarial positions were filled; we still have one vacant position. Our staff as of the end of 1981 numbers five permanent and three temporary correspondence secretaries.

Personal Activities

On December 5, I spent the afternoon at our branch office in Burbank as the guest of Louise Smythe, manager of the center. I thought it would be worthwhile to familiarize myself with their systems and procedures, and I came back with a number of good ideas. (I'll report on them as they are implemented.)

I recently celebrated my five-year anniversary with the company and enjoyed a pleasant lunch with Bob Anderson, director of personnel.

See the difference? When you arrange your information in categories, you and your reader can easily spot the specific tasks you have worked on during the month. And the category setup gives you a built-in mechanism for follow-up: What wasn't completed will be carried over to the next month; what was completed can drop off and make room for the next project.

The progress report can have another function, besides highlighting your activities—it can be the bearer of bad news. But bad news should not and cannot be kept a secret, at least not for a long time. In some cases, it is better to reveal the bad news and face it squarely than to have it brought to management's attention through other indirect sources (consider yourself lucky if you haven't been burnt by the grapevine method of communication).

And sometimes you can make bad news work for you in a positive way—by being prepared to meet it, react to it, and rechannel it. For example, the chief executive officer of a major cosmetics company requires department heads to identify specific trouble spots. These are described to him in a form of communication known as "action alerts," and the bad-news bearer is required to explain it, have a plan for correcting it, and be prepared to correct it within a reasonable amount of time. Now this may sound unappealing, to be sure, but if you're a clever manager you will be prepared and won't be caught off guard without a plan.

It isn't enough to know what needs to be done; you have to know how to put it into action. And as long as someone can be confident that you are on top of it, that you know how to handle this problem, then you will be able to continue with a vote of confidence under your belt. And when you know and show you're in control by anticipating trouble spots, you take away one less item for management to be worried about—and voila! another positive impact!

Just one more method of making an impact through written presentations and then we'll move on to examine oral presentation forms.

Minutes of Meetings

Some meetings you attend are formal ones—maybe a group of people meet regularly as a committee or a task force to discuss problems and resolve ideas. These meetings may have a designated secretary who will record the topics discussed at the meeting and create an official report of the business transacted. This official report is known as the minutes of the meeting.

Minutes comprise an official record and, for that reason, have specific parts, headings, and formats.

But what about an unofficial impromptu meeting; or a conference to plot strategy for a client's advertising campaign; or a meeting to firm up plans for new filing procedures in your department? Should those meetings have recorded minutes? Or what about these situations: You attend a two-day seminar on supervisory techniques; or a three-and-a-half-day regional conference for all planning directors; or a luncheon meeting at which the speaker talks about impending legislation that might affect your building plans?

My question is, no matter what reason for the meeting and no matter how much or little time was involved, how are you going to report your findings? Or are you even going to report your findings?

Of course you are; we know that by now. But you may need a bit of help in deciding what to report and how to report it. So let's establish some guidelines:

- If you attend a class (seminar/workshop/conference) in order to expand or improve your own capabilities, tell others.
- If you attend a meeting (class/workshop/conference) and decisions are made that have a bearing on other people or departments, tell them.
- If you attend a workshop (class/meeting/conference) that

would be of interest to others, tell them.
• If you learned something at a seminar (class/workshop/ meeting) that is worthy of being passed on, tell others.

Now you know when to tell, but what do you tell?

If your meeting is a regularly scheduled one and a formal one, then the minutes should follow a special format that includes the names of committee members, the names of people making motions and seconding them, the exact wording of motions, and a record of all reports and motions. Less formal meetings or conferences you attend do not follow such a prescribed format, but summaries of topics discussed and decisions made should be included.

We will explore the formal and informal ways of preparing and presenting meeting summaries, but both methods have similar objectives:

Objectives of Minutes

1. To present information to keep management and key staff members informed of significant happenings
2. To present a summary of topics discussed, including main resolutions, unfinished business, and who is to carry out the issues
3. To record the decisions made concerning any issues
4. To provide as much information as is necessary to keep others aware of important matters

How to Assemble Formal Minutes of Meetings

Minutes represent the official record of the proceedings of a meeting. Minutes have two major purposes: to create an official record of a meeting, and to summarize the business conducted at a meeting.

Some minutes of meetings may be more thorough and formal than others, especially when legal requirements must be met, but all minutes of formal meetings should include this information:

1. A heading with:
   - Name of the committee or type of meeting or task force
   - The words *Minutes of the* _____ *Meeting*
   - Date of the meeting
   - Names of those attending the meeting
   - Names of those absent from the meeting

2. A statement describing the group holding its meeting tement describing the group holding its meeting (name of facility)   on ___(date and time)___.

3. A statement that the meeting was called to order by __(chairperson, president, person in charge)__ and that the minutes of the previous meeting were distributed and a motion was made to approve or amend them.

A formal regularly scheduled meeting will have an agenda of the topics to be discussed or reported on at the meeting. Each topic discussed can be summarized in its own separate paragraph. You don't have to provide a word-for-word summary of what was discussed. What you want to aim for is an outsider's understanding of the main topics discussed and resolved; or, if there is no resolution, then a clear understanding of who is to accomplish what by the next meeting.

When a formal motion is made, however, to carry out an activity or to propose a formal vote, then the accepted language for making motions must be used. The correct language for stating motions should include the name of the party making the motion and the party who seconds it, and the written motion should be stated in that order.

Minutes should be unbiased — there should not be any comments about the quality or quantity of the topics discussed; so statements such as "Jon Simmons and Kathleen Vogel had a heated discussion about the price of the tickets for the employee banquet" should be written as "Jon Simmons and Kathleen Vogel discussed the price of the tickets for the employee banquet."

Minutes should end with an announcement about the time and date of the next meeting and should state the time the present meeting was adjourned.

For the record then, minutes of meetings should include this information:

- The action taken
- Who is to carry out the action
- Who is to make a report—and by what date
- What is left unfinished or pending
- Motions and resolutions
- Motion maker and motion seconder by name
- Summaries of topics discussed
- Notice of meeting adjournment and announcement of next meeting

Here's a sample of what minutes look like:

Policy and Procedure Review Committee

Minutes of regular meeting held March 5, 1981

Members in Attendance	*Members Absent*
Kathleen Ambrose, chairperson	none
Donna J. Carson, floating member	
Marcia Conley	
David Iwana	
Joan Kardis	

1. Call to Order

The weekly meeting of the Policy and Procedure Review Committee was called to order by Kathleen Ambrose, chairperson, at 2:30 P.M. in the tenth floor conference room.

2. Previous Minutes

The minutes of the previous meeting were read. David Iwana made a motion to approve them, seconded by Marcia Conley.

3. Increased Committee Membership

The committee discussed the need to increase the membership from four to six permanent members. Several names of potential members were raised, and a motion was made by Joan Kardis and seconded by Marcia Conley to ask Susan Hedges and Ethel Washington to serve on the committee. Backup choices are Nora Donnelly and Frank Hayes.

Kathleen Ambrose volunteered to approach these people and request their voluntary assistance on the committee. She will report on their acceptance at the next meeting.

4. Meeting Time Change

Donna Carson suggested that the meeting time be changed to 4:00 P.M. The committee members decided that this decision should be made by the full committee, so a final discussion and decision will take place when the new committee members have joined.

5. Committee Responsibilities

The responsibilities of the committee officers were agreed upon:

- The chairperson will prepare a monthly report of the committees' activities and submit it to the director of operations.
- The chairperson will write the cover memo to be distributed with any new or revised procedure.
- The secretary will furnish minutes of each meeting to the committee members the day before the next meeting.
- The secretary will develop an agenda for the upcoming meeting and distribute it to all committee members.

6. Approval of Procedures

All procedures must have the final approval of the committee before they can be issued. This motion was made by Joan Kardis and seconded by David Iwana.

7. Next Meeting

Kathleen Ambrose announced that the next regular meeting will take place on March 12, 1981.

8. Adjournment

The meeting was adjourned at 3:30 P.M.

Submitted by _____
                              Secretary

How to Condense an Abundance of Information

You might be thinking that minutes are easy to compile for those formal structured meetings. What about the instances where you have an informal group discussion to discuss a problem? Or you attended a seminar to improve your skills? Or you participated in a strategy planning session?

If you want to have a documented record of what issues were discussed and resolved, if you want to keep others informed of these decisions and your activities, then write a meeting report. Your report doesn't have to be formally arranged with attendees, times, motions, etc.; what you want to get across is a summary of the items discussed, problems encountered, and tasks assigned.

These meeting reports can summarize everything from a personal conference you attended to one at which hundreds of people were in the audience. You may be asked to prepare a report by your superiors; or you may take it upon yourself to write one. Whatever the reason, you will always want to include a summary of discussions and decisions.

A meeting report can be organized just like any other report or memo you would write; this time your headings would be organized around topics discussed. For instance, you might have headings such as:

- Purpose of the meeting
- Goals and objectives

- Topics discussed (outlined by topic)
- Follow-up action to be taken
- Personal benefits gained from the meeting

This summary can be prepared and presented in memo format, as in this example:

To: Ben Blokland
From: George Anderson
Re: Summary of Data Processing Forum—held in San Francisco, January 19, 1982

Objectives of the Forum

The company's data processing divisions held their second forum in San Francisco last month. Members of the management group agreed to these overall objectives:

1. To maintain the longevity of the forum
2. To provide for the technological exchange of information, with primary emphasis on "how to" rather than plain results
3. To expand the understanding of users about the key elements in planning for data processing needs

Items Discussed

A number of issues related to achieving these objectives were discussed:

1. Common sources of data
2. User involvement and interface
3. Tools and techniques for acquiring data
4. Basic systems configurations
5. Highlights of efforts made to accomplish effective planning

Action to Be Taken

Several areas were identified as requiring specific actions

by the forum attendees. These actions and the person responsible are identified below:

Action	Party Responsible
1. Promote user involvement	George Anderson
2. Develop an interview plan for acquiring data	Fred Warren
3. Write a program describing basic systems	Harriet Shaw
4. Collect materials relating to user problems	Marge Fox and P. J. Duran

Overall, I feel the meeting was most informative, and excellent attention was directed at some of our common problems. I can see a lot of benefits to be derived from our involvement in this group.

We meet again next month, and I'll keep you posted on the progress we make.

A True Story about Writing Reports of Meetings

Most of us workers attend at least one meeting a day. Some are worthwhile, but some make us wonder why we ever left our desks in the first place. What usually happens though, even at the worthwhile meetings, is that a number of issues get assigned and resolved verbally, but the follow-up mechanism is in our heads. Now what are the odds of each person at the meeting remembering everything to do as well as everything others are to do?

This point was most impressively brought home to me when I received a little memo one afternoon describing the activities of a meeting I had attended that morning. There it was — staring me in the face — a record of everything we had discussed and what action we planned. And I knew if I had a copy of the information, so did everyone else at the meeting have that same reminder.

I was impressed! I asked the writer about her reasons for distributing a summary of our meeting — after all, this is a situation where writing means more work and no one had specifically requested minutes. So if I can paraphrase her words after all this time (I know, I know, I should have taken notes), her reasons for summarizing meetings were:

- To document what was discussed and what action would be taken
- To have a record of what was agreed to by the people present
- To have a reminder of what items need follow up
- To impress people with her competency

Yes, she made no bones about it — she was out to prove her competency by putting it in writing. And if you are after the same goal, you'll start doing the same thing. Need I say any more about the power of the written word?

V. Oral Presentations

You've got to be kidding: Me talk to a group?!

Who's kidding? Talking to a group is serious business. It's so serious that a majority of people rate public speaking as their biggest fear—and that's over snakes and the dark!

But this fear of public speaking is usually unfounded. Or, to phrase that another way: You are never as bad as you think you are.

To illustrate . . . One of the seminars I conduct is called "Overcoming the Fear of Speaking." Everyone in the group is there for a very specific reason: They are all terrified of speaking, some to a group of people, some in one-on-one situations. Most of the people will do anything to avoid public speaking—they telephone, they write, they send messages, they have stand-ins. But somewhere along the line these people have got to be personally accountable and meet with others. And they realize that if they don't do something about their fear, their personal and professional lives are at a standstill.

The first exercise we try is to have each person introduce himself or herself to the group from the front of the room and to discuss their own personal speaking fears. Later in the seminar each person relates a story or personal experience or some information for a couple of minutes. Then I ask how that individual feels at that moment, and the feelings expressed range from sweating palms, shaking knees, cracking voice, flushed face, wildly beating heart, to other assorted body signals. But the people listening to the speaker always say, "Really? You seemed so calm; you didn't look at all nervous. Your voice was even, your legs were steady, you seemed in control."

And they really were in control. As the innocent observer in the back of the room I can vouch for their appearance. Honest, they didn't project the innermost fears they thought they were projecting.

Not convinced yet? May I offer another illustration...

In one of these "Overcoming the Fear of Speaking" sessions, a twenty-three-year old woman chose as her exercise to describe her experience in climbing Mt. Kilimanjaro, the highest mountain in Africa, to a height of over 19,000 feet. She told us of her preparation, her fears, her determination, her exhaustion, her will to succeed, and her exhilaration in reaching the top of the mountain. I listened, spellbound by her achievement, but disturbed by her lack of self-assurance in being able to talk comfortably to the group.

So I asked the obvious question: "How could you climb Mt. Kilimanjaro but be frightened about talking to us today?" (After all, I felt we were contrasting life and death versus no threat of death situations.) She answered that she had felt thoroughly prepared for her climbing expedition and was competing against herself, but in speaking she felt unprepared and that she would be judged by others.

These are the two major fears for the speaker: the fear

of being unprepared and the fear of being negatively judged by others.

Are these fears real? Certainly they are, if you are experiencing them. But are they necessary? No, because you will be prepared to speak and because you have a valuable message to convey to your listeners.

But the big question is: How to keep from having these fears?

First of all, always have a sure grasp of your subject matter—your knowledge will give you a necessary cushion of comfort. If you're prepared to discuss your subject, you will feel secure knowing that you are an expert and can talk authoritatively about it. Your audience is looking for information and assumes you can provide it; be prepared to share your knowledge and they won't be disappointed—and you won't be either.

And when you have that sure grasp of your subject matter, how will your audience be able to put a negative judgment on you? That's right—they can't! Look at it this way: An audience doesn't walk into the room thinking thoughts of failure for you. The audience doesn't want you to make a fool of yourself; they are on your side and rooting for your success. And they stay on your side until you prove them wrong—but you won't do that.

Informal and Formal Talks

This feeling of being afraid to talk in front of others is a common one, but it's not as hopeless a situation as you might think. You will probably, in your personal and professional encounters, have to speak to others. Sometimes it will be relatively easy—a casual conversation with a friend describing some costly but necessary home improvement plans; other times it will be a bit harder—telling your boss about a new procedure you would like to test, or convincing a group of colleagues to ditch the proposed program and start again.

Whatever the situation, there's always one thing you can count on . . . the feeling that it's you against them.

My first bit of advice, if you find yourself in that situation, is to turn the negative feeling into a positive one. Ask yourself: "What are the needs of my audience? What do they want to hear?"

You might be thinking, This is the same advice she gave me about writing an effective memo. You're right! The advice is the same: Whether you speak it or write it, think of your audience first—because a presentation is a presentation.

How to Make a Powerful Oral Presentation

You've reached that point of no return—you have to talk to others. Like it or not, you're in the middle of it, so you better give them your best shot.

Look at it this way: If you think your idea is good, then you should *want* to tell others; or if the request to make a presentation comes from others, would they ask you to do it if they didn't think you could?

Let's concentrate on the tools and techniques you can use when making an on-the-job presentation: for the kinds of situations in which you have to present some ideas to a committee or make a convincing argument to a group of people; for an informal gathering of people to whom you will speak somewhat extemporaneously, using notes if you like but certainly not a prepared memorized speech; and in the kinds of presentations where you will feel comfortable, natural, and involved with your audience—the best kind.

I have spoken to groups of two to several hundred. Give me a small group anytime! I like audience participation, questions and comments, and immediate feedback to tell me whether I'm getting through or not. People will ask me, "How do you do it? How do you talk to a group?" And often I do indeed wonder how I do it! Because it isn't an easy thing to do, and I would by no means tell you it's an easy thing to do. But I will tell you this, and I'll refer back to the Masters and Johnson approach, if I may borrow an analogy: You do get better the more you practice. And, as Masters and Johnson advocate, practice a lot because practice is fun!

Take it one step at a time. If you start out testing your oral presentation techniques on small groups, soon you'll feel comfortable enough to move on to bigger ones.

Now for those techniques I promised . . .

1. First get organized in your mind:

- What attitude or action do you want your audience to take after hearing your presentation?
- Do you want to inform, instruct, convince, gain support, or some combination of these?

2. Decide on the most workable format for your presentation—for your audience as well as for yourself:

- Is it an informal meeting, where people will feel comfortable about exchanging views and asking questions?
- Would you prefer that the audience hold all their questions until after your presentation?
- Is the group so large that audience participation isn't possible?
- Do you want to work with visual aids?

3. Analyze your audience:

- What does the audience want to hear?
- What benefits can you point out so the audience will want to listen?

- What kind of people are you talking to: visual, cost-concerned, humorless, time-conscious, etc.?

4. Gather your thoughts, using one of these methods:

- Speak into a tape recorder, without worrying about order; work from the transcribed copy to arrange your ideas in priority order.
- Write out your entire presentation, arranging and editing just as you would for any written document.
- Make notes on index cards, with one or two notes to a card, to help remind you of the important points you want to cover.

You'll recall that we covered these same steps when we learned how to make a written presentation. And our next step after organizing is to prepare. The preparation method you choose will depend upon how skilled you are as a speaker and how comfortable you are addressing a group.

Whichever method you choose, keep in mind that you want to be able to face your group confidently. There is absolutely nothing wrong with taking note cards with you and referring to them while you are talking. But you run several risks when you memorize or read your talk word-for-word from a paper: If you forgot a line, would you be able to recover quickly and ad-lib until your memory returned? If you lost your reading place, would you be calm enough to find your place again? If someone interrupted with a question, could you answer it and then smoothly get yourself and your audience back to the place where you left off?

If you go in with a prepared text, you had better be prepared for and be able to handle mishaps and interruptions. I think you'll find that's why many speakers prefer to work from good notes to remind them of what they want to say rather than tell them what they want to say.

5. Prepare your talk: Write, outline, or note enough information as you'll need to help you get started and carry you through.

6. "Write" your presentation:

a. The Beginning
   • Identify yourself and your connection to the group or topic.
   • Describe the subject of your presentation.
   • Mention how your audience will benefit from listening to you.
b. The Middle
   • Present the bulk of your information, using your outline, note cards, and any visual aids.
   • Aim for smooth transitions from one point to the next.
c. The End
   • Review the highlights of your presentation.
   • Present a summary of ideas.
   • Call for an action, if that was your purpose.
   • Make a circle—come back to your original statement of what was to be accomplished from your presentation.

In other words, your presentation should start out and end by accomplishing your purpose; if you can do that, come full circle, then you will know your presentation was an organized and effective one.

How to Exhibit Poise in Front of a Group

So you're scared about an upcoming presentation you have to make; that's okay—just don't wait until the last minute to find out how you look and sound to the group. Try out your presentation on a friend, a spouse, or a business associate. If this is too unnerving or embarrassing, and it can be, then stand before a mirror and practice your talk.

1. Talk to your audience:

• Use words and references they can understand.
• Avoid jargon and technical terminology.

2. Polish your vocal delivery:

• Emphasize important points with your voice.
• Check your breathing stress points. Speak in short words and short sentences so you won't get out of breath.
• Change your speaking speed according to the complexity of your material; speed up for the easy parts; slow down for the harder parts.
• Change your voice pitch so that you don't put yourself and your audience to sleep with a monotonous voice.
• Practice the pause; you don't have to fill every space with a sound—silence is a pleasure sometimes, especially instead of running words together.
• Be aware of how many times you say "um," "er," "uh," and other assorted space fillers; we usually make these sounds without thinking, especially when we're trying to gather our next thoughts. These sounds can be grating to the ear and, if nothing else, are not necessary.
• Avoid running words together; give your audience time to digest what they heard.

3. Be aware of your own body language:

• Engage in definite eye contact with members of the audience.
• Stand in a relaxed fashion. Hands in pockets are okay, as long as you're not jingling change or tugging at the material.
• Use your hands and arms to emphasize your points, not to detract from them.

- Move about naturally—don't pace back and forth or, worse, stand dead still.
- Watch out for nervous gestures: drumming pencils, destroying paper clips, touching hair, adjusting clothes, and other assorted nervous habits. These can only draw your audience's attention away from what you're saying to what you're doing.

These last pointers about body language are so important because you want to appear outwardly comfortable and relaxed, even though your insides may be like jelly. And it's important to get an observer's opinion because you may not even be aware of any nervous gestures. Let me tell you a story about how these gestures can detract from the force of your words. . . .The leader of a workshop I attended had a distracting habit of constantly tucking her hair behind her ear, which kept falling in front of her face. I became fascinated by the playfulness of her hair, almost losing contact with her words and intentions. And I wondered how many others in my group were paying attention to her hair instead of her words.

She happened to be discussing presentation techniques, specifically distracting habits and nervous gestures. Several in the group called out, "But you're doing it with your hair" and "I haven't been listening; I've been watching your hair."

The cynical part of me wondered if she had been making this movement purposely, but she was genuinely surprised by the comments and completely unaware of her gestures. Of course, she made a trooper's attempt after that to pay no attention to her hair or, at the most, to tuck it behind occasionally, but you knew she was always aware of it and always a little uncomfortable.

And speaking of being uncomfortable . . .

4. Choose clothing that is comfortable and flattering, and that won't get in the way of your presentation. That way you'll know how it feels, how it looks, and whether it's right for the occasion. Try on your clothes at least one day before your presentation so you'll know if your shirt buttons

are ready to pop from too many big lunches, or if your jacket is spotted from those same lunches. The less you have to be concerned about or upset about, especially over a controllable item like clothing, the calmer you will be.

So, the big moment finally arrives; there's no way to put it off any longer; you have to go out there and face them.

How to Relax and Have a Good Time

This is it—the point of no return; you've got to address that audience, whether you want to or not. But let me give you some realistic ways of dealing with your anxiety and some suggestions for making the best presentation you can.

1. Get to the site early so you can familiarize yourself with the room arrangement, set up your materials, or get acquainted with the group. I like to get to the presentation site early to mingle with the people as they arrive; if there's coffee or refreshments, even better— then we can get acquainted in a casual way. I introduce myself as the speaker, and we talk about anything— the weather, the traffic, the news—anything to help me establish a feeling of camaraderie with some members of the group. When the time comes for me to address the group, I can spot several friendly and compassionate faces in the crowd—these are the ones I discussed freeway traffic with, poured coffee with, and felt empathy from when I said I was the speaker. The more friends you can gather on your side before you begin, the fewer you'll have to win over while you're talking—that's for sure.

2. Tell yourself you can do it:

   - Take a deep breath.
   - Clear your head.
   - Concentrate on your goal.

3. Be convincing and enthusiastic. Point out benefits to your audience.
4. Be interested in your subject, and let it show.
5. Sprinkle your presentation with appropriate stories, examples, and bits of humor:

   - Your stories and examples must be relevant to your group and their experiences.
   - Try out your humorous examples before relating them. What is humorous to you might not be humorous to others.

6. Be aware of your audience's body language:

   - Watch for puzzled expressions on faces.
   - Check for head movements. Is the audience agreeing or disagreeing with you? (Look for up and down (yes) or side to side (no) movements.)
   - React to signs of unrest or boredom. It could be time to change your tactics, or at least consider your audience's limitations.

7. Encourage or anticipate questions. Be prepared to know what your audience will want to know.
8. Present some ideas in the form of questions. Make your audience want to respond to your ideas.
9. Be aware of your facial expressions. Smile!
10. Make a positive first impression:

    - Project warmth and understanding.
    - Show that you're human.

11. Remember that you are in control:

    - You are the leader and can control when the audience speaks and for how long.
    - Keep that control—and get it back if it starts to get away from you.
    - You are the expert and the audience is rooting for your success.

12. Take the opportunity to make oral presentations as often as you can — you will get better!

People will listen to you if you feel you're worth listening to. Projecting that positive and confident attitude is what makes a good speaker.

How to Use Visual Aids

Visual aids to use in a presentation can take any of these forms:

- blackboard
- easel and flip chart
- hand-out materials
- magazine articles
- charts and graphs
- overhead projector
- slides

Visual aids can certainly enhance your presentation, but they can't substitute for it. A good speaker knows that visual aids are tools for highlighting information or for providing background justification for the ideas presented, but the speaker is still the main focal point in the presentation.

Here are some suggestions on how to use visual aids to your advantage:

1. Get to the meeting site early to get yourself calmly ready for your presentation. Make sure all the supplies you need are available and in working order (chalk, copies of materials, projector, pads and pencils).

2. Draw or write information on the blackboard or easel before the presentation begins, if possible. This will save time and keep you from losing direct contact with your audience.

3. Talk to your audience — not to your chart. People lose

interest and comprehension drops when they can't "see" what the speaker is saying. Stand to the side of your chart, with most of your body still facing the group. Point to items of interest on the chart, but then immediately return to eye contact with the audience.

4. Point out special features or interesting aspects of the chart. Don't repeat the obvious; your audience can read the column headings and the figures — tell them something new. For example, let's say you're discussing some sales figures for the past six months. Two columns on the chart look like this:

Month	Machines Sold
January	25
February	31
March	32
April	10
May	32
June	35

Which version would your audience like to hear:

> In January we sold twenty-five machines, in February we increased to thirty-one, and stayed about the same in March. In April there was a dramatic drop because of a trade embargo with our importer, but our May figures were back in line.

or

> You'll notice a dramatic decrease in the number of machines sold in April; this resulted from a trade embargo with our importer. But we were able to recover in May and have continued to see an increase since then.

5. Keep your charts clean, clear, and easy to understand. Avoid cramming too much information into one chart—

limit it to essential information, or use two charts.

6. Distribute hand-out materials during your presentation only when you want the audience to read or examine the materials right then. Otherwise the audience may focus attention on the materials rather than on what you're saying. If the materials are for reference purposes, then distribute them at the end of the meeting, or have the audience pick up copies as they leave.

7. Give your audience a few moments to become familiar with hand-out materials. You'll lose your audience if you continue talking while materials are being distributed. Use them as you would any other visual aid. Point out special interest items or expand on the contents; don't just merely read what's written.

How to Handle Questions

You're up there at the front of the room and you're doing just fine: After a few unsettling moments your stomach stopped fluttering and you began to relax and get into your topic; you're maintaining eye contact, even remembering to smile occasionally; your charts look good; the projector hasn't broken down; and the audience is still awake. So far so good.

But your heart rate rises again—there's a hand raised in the back of the room, and you have to acknowledge it. Is it the question you have been dreading, hoping no one would ask it? It is! But you smile and say, "I'm glad you asked that," and you answer it coolly and correctly, and the questioner is satisfied with your explanation.

Here are some tips for handling questions:

1. Be prepared. Anticipate the kinds of questions your audience will ask. Think about how you would answer these questions; formulate some responses.

2. Be honest. If you don't know or don't have the answer, say so. Don't hesitate or fake it; the audience is sensitive

to this and will quickly realize it. You can lose points for faking information.

3. Present some of your ideas in the form of questions—the audience will be drawn to respond.

4. Ask the audience to write their questions on cards. Collect them and then you choose the ones you want to answer. (I'm not a big fan of this technique, preferring the extemporaneous question, but some people swear by it; and it's a good way, when you're starting out, to get used to answering questions. Watch Johnny Carson answer questions this way from the audience—he's a master at it.)

Some final words: Have a good time while you're up there. Have a sense of humor and let your personality show through; otherwise, you may come off like a block of wood. And people will say, "Wait a second. I know she's not like that, she seemed so uptight and rigid. That's not the way she usually is in informal situations."

By letting some of your personality show through, people get a sense of who you are and what you are, and that's what people respond to. If you exhibit a down-to-earth mentality, it will be easier for you to communicate with people.

I don't know if you're going to dash out tomorrow and volunteer to make a presentation to three hundred people, but try it with a small group and keep perfecting your techniques. Pretty soon you'll hear comments such as these: Bravo! Dynamic speaker! She made it so interesting! Tell us more!

Twenty-five Hot Tips for Making a Powerful Oral Presentation

1. Get organized in your mind. What attitude or action do you want the audience to take?
2. Decide on a workable format for your presentation.
3. Analyze your audience.

4. Gather your thoughts on tape or in writing.
5. Prepare your talk. Use an outline or note cards.
6. "Write" your presentation.
7. Talk to your audience in language they can understand.
8. Polish your vocal delivery.
9. Be aware of your body language.
10. Choose a comfortable and flattering outfit to wear.
11. Get to the speaking site early to familiarize yourself with the room arrangement.
12. Tell yourself you can do it.
13. Be convincing and enthusiastic.
14. Be interested in your subject, and let it show.
15. Sprinkle your presentation with appropriate stories, examples, and humor.
16. Use visual aids to enhance your presentation.
17. Talk to your audience—not to your charts.
18. Let your audience have a few moments to become familiar with hand-out materials.
19. Be aware of your audience's body language.
20. Encourage or anticipate questions—be prepared.
21. Present some ideas in the form of questions.
22. Be aware of your facial expressions. Smile!
23. Make a positive first impression.
24. Remember that you are in control.
25. Take the opportunity to make oral presentations as often as you can—you will get better!

Meetings

"He's in a meeting."
"Why don't we get together and talk this over?"
"Got a few minutes?"

"Let's take this up at the weekly staff meeting."

"How can I get everything done? I'm always going to meetings."

Expressions such as these are heard in offices and coffee shops around the world. Wherever people gather and work together, you can count on some sort of a meeting to take place.

Meetings can take a variety of forms: They can range from an informal gathering of two or three people to formal arrangements of committee members or department members. The purposes may range from exchanging information to devising and implementing new decisions to boosting morale.

Certain behavior takes place at these meetings, and it might be a good idea to examine this behavior so we can better understand how to make an impact at meetings.

How to Develop an Agenda for Meetings

That's rule No. 1. Always have an agenda of the subjects that will be discussed at the meeting. If it does nothing else but keep the discussion on the necessary subjects and away from secondary or irrelevant ones, you will at least feel satisfied about keeping a meeting from getting off the track.

The agenda should list the items or points that will be discussed at the meeting. Some of these items may be continuations of unfinished business from previous discussions; some may be new business. Usually the person requesting the meeting, or chairing it in the case of formal meetings, decides on the items to be included on the agenda. Requests for other items to be included on the agenda should be given to the agenda organizer well before the meeting so that they can be included.

You can also use an agenda as an outline for your presentation; this will be useful to the audience, who can thus follow along with your talk and will have an outline of your talk to take with them.

Setting Up an Agenda

1. Have an agenda that lists the items or points to be covered at a meeting. An agenda helps to keep a meeting going along an organized course.

2. Use an agenda as an outline for your presentation. The audience can follow along with your presentation and will have it for later reference.

3. Arrange agenda items in priority order—the most important items should be treated first.

4. Place those items that require creative thinking high on the list. The group's energy and interest are highest at the start of a meeting, and go downward from there. If any items need creative thinking and high-level interaction, place them toward the top of the agenda.

5. Include items that are of interest to everyone at the meeting. This technique will help you maintain the group's interest and feeling of unity. Treat items of interest to only one or two people in separate sessions.

6. Decide on an appropriate amount of time for each discussion item. Note the time allotment on the agenda. This tenchique will help you and the group stay on the

7. Give people an idea of the approximate time the meeting will end.

8. Be aware of the items to be discussed and whether they will have positive or negative effects on the audience. You might want to start with the "bad news" and move on to "good news"; or you might want to arrange it in "good, bad, good" fashion. It's usually a good idea to end the meeting on a positive note.

9. Think strategy—don't just haphazardly list the items for discussion.

10. Issue the agenda in advance of the meeting: For a formal meeting, send the agenda two or three days before the meeting so the audience can become familiar with the discussion items; for an informal meeting, send the agenda one day before the meeting; if there are just one

or two items, you can probably send the agenda as part of a memo confirming your meeting.

How to Conduct a Meeting

Okay, you now have a well-developed agenda. How do you conduct the meeting?

1. Begin the meeting on time. If a meeting is called for 2:00 P.M., then it begins at 2:00 and not at 2:07 to give the people coming from another office time to get there.

This point was effectively brought home to me at a seminar scheduled to begin at 9:30 A.M. I looked at the clock and said, "Let's give it a few more minutes before starting." (Twelve out of twenty-one people were there.) One man asked, "Why do those of us on time always have to wait for the latecomers? Why aren't we rewarded by starting as scheduled and the others penalized by missing the information?" And you know what? He is right. Since then, I have always begun and appeared for a meeting at the designated time.

2. Stick to the items on the agenda. If you have indicated time allocations, try not to exceed them.

3. Encourage discussion among members of the group. Call for participation from some of the more silent members. ("Can you see any problems with this decision in your area, Ann?" or "Tom, tell us about the system you've just introduced.")

4. Summarize the information presented and call for decisions if necessary.

Sounds ideal doesn't it? Everything goes according to plan, everyone behaves appropriately and positively, and the meeting ends on a happy note. Utopia, you say? What company is this? I should sit in on a meeting at your place?

Okay, you're right. What's the expression? . . . Put two people together and you have a discussion; three people and you have an argument.

So your meeting is proceeding all right, but that's because the boss isn't around so people are feeling more comfortable about suggesting ideas. Or Mr. Bigmouth is on vacation this week. Or the steady talker was finally told to keep quiet.

This brings us to our next topic . . .

How to Keep the Discussion Appropriate

Watch out for people—they'll be the downfall of your meeting. But what else is a meeting but an assembly of people? Fortunately, there are techniques for handling them skillfully and tactfully so that the meeting stays productive.

1. Firmly control the talkers:
   - Reassert the time allocation for the topic.
   - Reassert your leadership—
     a. Interrupt the speaker:
        - "I think that gives us enough information to make a decision on, Bill."
        - "You've raised some interesting points, Wayne. How do you feel about it, Gloria?"
     b. Verbally crowd the speaker:
        - 'Yes, that reminds me of a similar situation we faced last year."
     c. Hit 'em with a brick:
        - "Can we move on to the next agenda item?"
        - "We'll discuss this later if we have time."

2. Be aware of personal differences that can be the underlying cause of arguments:
   - Expand the discussion to include other members of the group.
   - Steer the discussion to the issues and away from the people.

3. Discourage the negative types who want to stifle ideas:
   - Encourage suggestions and praise the one who makes the suggestion.

- Discourage those who put down suggestions before they're even discussed or tried:
    - "Let's hear some more about this idea before rejecting it."

4. Bring the discussion back to the original issue as soon as it starts to get out of hand:
   - "Yes, what you said is valid, but we seem to be getting away from our primary purpose for meeting."

5. Listen attentively:
   - Keep your attention tuned to the speaker.
   - Watch for signs that the speaker is moving into the next gear—that could be the time to jump in and change tactics.
   - Listen for ideas, rather than facts.
   - Put aside emotional feelings and personal attitudes—concentrate on the issues.

6. Avoid taking sides; stop discussions headed in that direction.

7. Stress communication and the sharing of ideas.

Well, the meeting is really rolling along now, especially with your new people-pleasing techniques. How to end it?

How to Conclude a Meeting

1. Summarize the agenda items and any plans of action.

2. Close on a positive note:
   - Discuss the progress made.
   - Comment on the changes made, or the new plans, or the strengthened relationships.
   - Thank the group for their contributions.

3. Follow up with formal minutes or a summary memo of the items discussed, decisions reached, and actions to be taken.

Two Dozen Tips On How To Plan and Conduct a Meeting

1. Have an agenda that lists the items or points to be covered at a meeting.
2. Use an agenda as an outline for your presentation.
3. Arrange agenda items in priority order; the most important items should be treated first.
4. Place agenda items requiring creative thinking high on the list. Cover them at the beginning, when the group's energy and interest are greatest.
5. Include items that are of interest to everyone, to ensure the group's attention and feeling of unity.
6. Decide on an approximate amount of time for each discussion item, and note the time allocation on the agenda.
7. Give people an idea of the approximate time the meeting will end.
8. Be aware of the items to be discussed and their positive or negative effect on the audience.
9. Think strategy—don't just haphazardly list the items for discussion.
10. Issue the agenda before the meeting so people will have an idea of the meeting's purpose.
11. Begin the meeting on time.
12. Stick to the items on the agenda.
13. Encourage discussions among members of the group.
14. Summarize the information presented and call for decisions if necessary.
15. Firmly control the talkers.
16. Be aware of personal differences that can be the underlying cause of arguments.
17. Discourage the negative types who want to stifle ideas.

18. Bring the discussion back to the original issue as soon as it starts to get out of hand.
19. Listen attentively; concentrate on the issues.
20. Avoid taking sides; stop discussions headed in that direction.
21. Stress communication and the sharing of ideas.
22. At the end of the meeting, summarize agenda items and any plans of action.
23. Close on a positive note; refer to the progress the group members have made, and thank them for their contributions.
24. Follow up with formal minutes or a summary memo of the items discussed, decisions reached, and actions to be taken.

Telephone

Mention the word *telephone* and people collect on four sides of the room — some swear by it, others view it as a necessary evil; some never use it, others would be dead without it.

There's no use denying the existence of the telephone. Whatever your personal feelings are about the telephone, you can learn to use it to your advantage.

When to Reach for the Telephone

Use the telephone to:

- start the ball rolling
- exchange instant information
- save time, when time is short
- make appointments — or break them if you must

The telephone carries with it the idea of speed: all those wonderful words of ours, magically carried over trunks, cables, and wires to locations hundreds, sometimes thousands, of miles away. But for what purpose?—to bring us closer to other human beings.

How to Handle Yourself Confidently and Competently on the Telephone

When you begin a telephone call, start by identifying yourself and your department (in whichever order is most recognizable). Do not pick up the phone and continue an ongoing conversation with someone in your office at the same time; it's rude and shows a lack of interest to the person on the other end of the line. When you pick up the telephone, make sure you are ready to talk to the person on the other end of the line.

Present your best side—if you placed the call, be prepared with an agenda; sometimes written, but usually an unwritten mental one. Always ask if this is a good time for this telephone conversation to be taking place—that gives the other party the option to talk at a more convenient time. If you receive the call and it's not a good time to talk, suggest a more appropriate time for the conversation. And if it's an unwanted call, let the caller down firmly and politely—perhaps suggesting another person the caller might try: "We have no need for this equipment, but you could try the finance department"; or "I'm sure your idea is very sound, but it's not something we would be interested in."

Let's assume that you're placing the call and the party on the other end answered the phone. What do you say? The standard scenario goes something like this:

> "Lifetime Guarantee Company."
> "May I speak to Mr. Shorter?"
> "May I say who's calling?"
> "This is Ms. Winter."
> "One moment please."

This sort of exchange must take place numerous times in every office every day. How can we improve upon it? Identify yourself as the caller, and combine that with your request:

> "Lifetime Guarantee Company."
> "This is Ms. Winter calling for Mr. Shorter."

This technique eliminates some unnecessary words, so you reach your party quickly, and, better yet, presents you as a professional.

When you have reached your party, begin by stating the purpose of your call:

- "I have those figures you requested. When would be a good time to go over them with you?"
- "We're almost out of the reversible belts advertised in today's sale. How soon can we get a repeat order?"
- "I'm compiling a report on executive compensation plans. Do you have any background information on other companies that I could use?"

In cases such as these, don't assume that the other person can and wants to drop ongoing work in order to talk to you and take care of your problem. Put yourself in the receiver's place and be ready to hear realistic answers:

- "I'll be tied up in meetings all afternoon. Why don't we get together tomorrow morning at 10:30?"
- "I'll need to call the factory and try to do some rearranging. Let me call you back later today or tomorrow morning for sure."
- "Yes. I do have some information you can use in your report, but it will take me some time to locate it. I'm getting ready for our annual sales convention next week. If you can wait until after the convention, I'll be glad to talk to you about this subject."

Use the telephone for short-term situations, for matters that can be settled quickly. Issues that are long, complicated, or delicate would probably be better explained in a letter or memo or treated at a personal meeting.

Another important point in handling yourself on the telephone is to listen attentively. Give the other person the respect and attention you expect for yourself. Repeat key points to be certain that you and the other party have the same understanding of the issues. Suspend judgment on what is said and listen to the issues.

And, most important, know when to end the conversation. Follow the advice of George Burns: "Say good night, Gracie." He always knew when to cut in: The audience was getting restless; Gracie's mind was wandering; time was running out; or it was just time to get off the stage.

Develop an awareness of the other party's inattention or impatience, through a variety of signals:

- Frequent mutterings and "uh-huhs" may indicate that the listener is occupied at another task.
- Low-voice phrases such as "Tell him I'll be with him in a minute" or "Ask her to stay on the line" indicate that the listener has other demands distracting from total attention to your call.
- Paper-rustling sounds may indicate that the listener is getting ready for a meeting or signing letters, or filling out an expense report—something other than listening.

Read the signals when you hear them and end the conversation before the other party ends it for you—you'll feel better.

Uses and Abuses of the Telephone

I read an amazing fact in a newspaper advertisement a couple of years ago, and I don't suppose the situation since then has improved: Eighty percent of business telephone calls are not completed on the first try—the person is out of the office, in a meeting, or unable to talk. And very often when the call is returned, the other party is unavailable. Is *everyone* out to lunch? And sometimes the first phone call isn't returned, so the caller tries again—again no luck. By this time our caller may begin to feel the first stages of paranoia. Sometimes the paranoia is justified; other times, there are reasons for unanswered telephone calls, such as:

1. The person didn't receive the message:
   - Please write down all messages you take, rather than relying on your memory.
   - Note the time of the call, and the caller's phone number.
   - Put the message in a spot where it will be seen.

2. The person is really tied up in meetings, conferences, and work-related activities:
   - Give the person some leeway in returning your call; it would be ideal if everyone returned our calls as soon as they walked into their offices, but that's unrealistic—give them a day or two.

3. The message is not clear and the person doesn't realize the need for returning the call:
   - Leave a distinct message, rather than just saying, "Ask her to give me a call."
   - Give more information: "I'd like to arrange a meeting to discuss some solutions to his inventory problems." "Could she call me by 3:00? I need this information for the committee meeting at 4:00."

There are, however, some situations in which not returning phone calls is *not* justified:

1. The person doesn't want to talk to the caller and hopes the caller will get the message:
   - This is positively unacceptable. Every human being deserves the courtesy of an answer, and you never know when the situation will be reversed.

2. The person uses silence as a way to screen out calls not worthy of attention:
   • This is also unacceptable—refer to previous explanation.

What should you do about unanswered calls, especially when you don't want to make a pest of yourself? If a reasonable amount of time has passed (one to three days) without a response, you have several alternatives to choose from:

1. Decide if you want to place another telephone call: Is the matter really important? Can you get the information elsewhere? Can you leave the information with another party?

2. If you place another phone call, make sure you leave a clear and complete message; for example, "I'd like to discuss the benefits proposal" or "Can he send a copy of the report to Jane Farlow in Merchandising? She would like to see the projections." Stay away from nonmessages such as "Ask him to give me a call."

3. Write a letter or memo instead of calling. The written word can have a greater impact than the telephone call; and besides, your audience will know what it is you want.

4. Drop the matter. Sometimes you have to just bite the bullet and forget about the matter (some situations are just not worth your time and aggravation).

5. Be ready when the person does eventually call you: Swallow your feelings and go on with business.

Now you can handle yourself confidently on the telephone. But how do you keep it from controlling your schedule?

How to Keep the Telephone Under Control

Do any of these sound familiar?

"If I could only turn off my phone."

"I can't get any work done—the telephone keeps interrupting me."

"Every time the phone rings I cringe and wonder what new problem awaits me."

"The telephone—I wish I didn't have one."

The telephone—one part ready access; one part constant nuisance. How to control it before it controls you?

First, remember that you do have control. You don't have to answer the telephone when it rings, you don't have to respond to every demand on your time, you don't have to accept the interruption. How, you ask? Here are three guidelines to follow:

1. Screen your phone calls:
   * Find out the caller's identity and the subject matter.
   * Determine if it's something that needs your immediate attention (remember—it's immediate to the caller but not necessarily to you).
   * Respond or delay, but base the decision on your own time constraints.
   * Ask your secretary or the person with telephone responsibility to get as much information from the caller as possible and to relay this information to you before talking to the caller.
   * Based on the information received and the caller's identity, handle the phone call (obviously when the chairman of the board or a valued superior calls and you are available, answer your phone).

2. Consolidate your calls:
   * Make as many phone calls as you can during the same set period of time, rather than making them individually.
   * Return as many phone calls as you can during the same set period of time, rather than returning them individually.
   * The time you set aside for making and returning telephone calls should be reasonable for both parties. Avoid

calling people during the times they might be out of the office (at lunch hours) or at the end of the work day.

3. Set up availability hours for phone calls:
   * Organize your day and your schedule according to specific hours for specific tasks—don't blend your activities.
   * Determine a schedule for yourself and stick to it.

Here's a success story to clarify what I'm proposing: I'm working with some supervisors at a health insurance company. The claims department gets bombarded with phone calls: 'What's happened to my claim?" "How much is insured?" "Why isn't this covered?" "When will I get my check?" And on and on and on. The claims manager and her supervisors can't get anything done because of the constant interruptions from claims processors and telephone inquiries.

My advice: (1) have all incoming phone calls screened and only the necessary major emergency calls directed to you; (2) have the information compiled by the person answering the phone; (3) research the information and answer the telephone inquiries during your availability hours; and (4) when you talk to people, express your interest and tell them you will get back to them between ____ and ____ (your availability hours, of course).

The results: a marked decrease in interruptions; an increase in getting work done; and a sense of relief related to feeling in control of time.

Remember—you have control over the telephone, not the other way around.

··
·   ·
·   *Hot Telephone Lines*   ·
·   ·
·   1. Use the telephone to: ·
·   • start the ball rolling   ·
··

- exchange instant information
- save time
- set appointments

2. Identify yourself and your business.
3. Begin a phone conversation only when you're ready—not when you're carrying on a conversation with another person in the room.
4. Be prepared with an agenda.
5. State the purpose of your call.
6. Find out if this is a convenient time to talk.
7. Use the telephone for short-term situations, for matters that can be settled quickly.
8. Listen attentively.
9. Know when to end the conversation.
10. Know when to follow up on an unanswered telephone call.
11. Decide whether to place another call, send a written message, or drop the matter entirely.
12. Screen your telephone calls.
13. Consolidate your telephone calls.
14. Set up times when you are available for phone calls.
15. Remember you have control over the phone; it doesn't control you.

Dictation

The dictating machine, like the telephone, has become a regular fixture in offices. Its presence is popping up everywhere: People carry pocket-sized ones and dictate while they're driving, while they're walking, and while they're working. That's the beauty of the handy portable machines—you can dictate anywhere.

Desk-top dictating machines have not been totally wiped out by the portable ones; and as more companies switch to centralized telephone dictation systems and word processing centers, the boss-speaking/secretary-writing method of dictation is becoming more and more obsolete.

Dictation is certainly a time saver—we all speak faster than we can write. And when we dictate we tend to use a more conversational, spoken style, so this makes our communications more personal.

Anything written can be dictated: letters, memos, and reports; minutes of meetings; travel itineraries and meeting schedules; instructions to be carried out; procedures.

If you're just beginning to dictate, you may want to start out with short and simple letters, and gain some confidence before moving on to more complex forms. But certainly add dictating skills to your business communications repertoire.

Here are some tips on how to dictate effectively.

How to Be a Dynamic Dictator

Proper dictation requires more talent than just turning on a machine and speaking into it. Planning is still a vital part of the process, just as it is when you write out the information fully. The difference in dictating is that you will cover all the preliminary steps but stop before the actual writing stage.

You can become a successful dictator by combining your communications know-how with your presentation skills—and practice.

Dictation can be broken down into three steps, as simple as a, b, c, but remember p, d, p:

A. Prepare

B. Deliver

C. Perfect

Prepare for Dictation

1. Gather your facts—get all the information you'll need for your message so that you can work without interruption:
   - Gather past correspondence from the files.
   - Consult with others about the situation.
   - Be prepared with names, addresses, dates, and figures.

2. Plan your message:
   - Jot down the important points to be covered.
   - Decide on your purpose for writing.
   - Plan your opening grabber and closing action.
   - Organize your points in priority order.

Deliver Your Dictation

1. Give instructions first. Before you begin dictating the actual document, give all necessary instructions to the transcriber:
   - Type of document
   - Type of stationery and envelope
   - Number of copies
   - Special handling or enclosures
   - Number of columns (if any)
   - Tabulations, lists, special margins
   - Information about mailing address, subject line, attention line
   - Prepare as a draft or final document

2. Make your message flow smoothly:
   - Visualize talking to the reader—strive for a natural-sounding tone.
   - Stop the machine when you are in doubt about a choice of words.

3. Speak clearly:
   - Speak slowly and distinctly so that words can be differentiated and understood.

- Stop the machine when you are thinking or forming thoughts.

4. Indicate punctuation, spelling, and other mechanics:
   - Spell proper names of people, companies, unusual terms when using them for the first time.
   - Indicate punctuation of commas, quotes, parentheses, periods, and new paragraphs.
   - Explain the use of columns, headings, indentations, and special formats.
   - Read columns of figures from left to right, not top to bottom.
   - If columns or tabulations are complicated, write them on paper instead of trying to explain them.
   - When giving instructions in the middle of dictation, start by saying "operator"; this will signal to the transcriber that the next words are instructions.
   - Indicate words to be underlined — after dictating, say, "operator, please underline beginning with the word _____."

Perfect Your Dictation

1. Listen to your dictation:
   - Play back your voice.
   - Listen to your dictation from *the transcriber's point of view*:
     - Are your instructions easy to follow?
     - Is your voice clear?
     - Does the message make sense?
     - Are there distracting noises (rustling papers, blowing smoke)?
     - Could you transcribe this document?

2. Practice your dictation:
   - Dictate as often as you can.
   - Dictate in those instances where you would normally reach for your yellow pad.
   - Keep on dictating — you will feel more comfortable with it.

3. Ask for feedback:
   • Ask the transcriber to comment on your dictation.
   • Ask for constructive criticism so you can improve your dictation skills and make it easier for the transcriber.

How to be a Dynamic Dictator

1. Gather your facts. Get all the information you need so you can work without interruption.
2. Plan your message. Decide on a purpose, organize important points, and plan opening and closing statements.
3. Give any special instructions before beginning the actual dictation.
4. Strive for a smooth flowing message.
5. Speak clearly and slowly so that your words can be understood.
6. Indicate punctuation, spelling, and other mechanics.
7. Listen to your dictation from the transcriber's point of view.
8. Practice your dictation.
9. Ask for feedback

VI. Follow Up

How to stay on top and ahead of your game!

Follow up—do you say you'll do it? Do you do it? Do you know how to provide for it?

Follow-up is taking that action a further step to gain more results, more sales, more referrals; and with it, you create an impression of competency and service. When you can do that, you gain a reputation and word spreads. You're building a base of people who will keep returning for your services because they respect and depend on your reliability and they enjoy doing business with you; they respond to your style; and they delight in the personal service.

Follow-up is a way of showing that you mean business. Every person is a salesperson—some sell products and some sell services. Mainly, though, you sell yourself. And what the other person needs to know is that you can produce, you want to please. How does that get communicated? When you do what you said you would do—when you follow up.

Follow-up shows you're concerned, you care—about the person, the product, and the results. When you follow up you're taking action, and that establishes a favorable impression with others.

If you can create a favorable impression, that information will be telegraphed. People will usually want to return for repeated contact and will usually refer your name to others. That's how business spreads and that's how you will get increased results.

If you're selling a product, follow-up lets people know that you're responsible, you are interested, and you can be trusted.

If you're providing a service, follow-up assures people that the job is being taken care of and, later, helps you find out if the job was carried out properly.

The Rationale Behind Achieving Results through Follow-up

- Do you find it easy to forget things you need to remember to do?
- Do you overlook informing others of your progress because you haven't made any?
- Do you run out of time to send thank-you letters?
- Has it been so long that you've forgotten what a thank-you letter is?

If your answer was yes to any of these questions, you're probably not following up. And if you're not following up, you're probably not achieving the best results. Relax, because help is here in the form of the follow-up program—a program to help you make an impact and achieve results in your particular profession.

The follow-up program for achieving success is based on proven methods that work for people like you. The biggest investment you'll be asked to make is one of time and commitment—a commitment to shape up your image for success.

The follow-up program is energy-efficient. It will help you trim the fat from your work habits, streamline your systems, and increase your productivity. The follow-up program is based on a system of reasons and rules, plans and programs—all helping to lead you to results. But it requires discipline; there aren't any shortcuts to success. You'll have to change your habits, discard the fat, and build up your reputation. But in the process you'll be reshaping your image and gaining on your goal of success.

How a Steady Follow-up Program Can Increase Your Success

Follow-up very often means doing something after the act, carrying the action another step so that you stretch your involvement. And when you stretch your involvement, you create a favorable impression of personalized business, personalized service. You gain a reputation for responsibility, for caring, and for taking the time. People take you seriously and respond to that extra dimension that sets you apart— you follow up.

A follow-up program can serve as your means for spreading your reputation and widening your contacts. You'll get referrals from it; you'll give referrals with it. You'll stay in control when temptation surrounds you.

The follow-up program can work for you and your needs. You'll develop new habits to help you stick to your program; you'll build up unused competency muscles; and you'll stabilize your schedule.

Basic Formulas for Achieving Results through Follow-up

Are you thinking that follow-up requires having a good memory and you don't have one? You already have too many things to do and don't need to make more work for yourself? That's probably true! And that's precisely why you need to develop a follow-up program that will help you control your information. Most of us try to follow up by remembering everything; or we make notes on small pieces of paper and then misplace the papers or get angry at all the clutter.

The point of a follow-up program is to be able to follow up regularly, at all times, and not just when you have a mental flash reminding you to check on an item that was due yesterday. Sometimes, though, we don't even see the possibility of using follow-up, so we need to develop some systems for helping us follow up. When you make it easy to follow up, you will follow up. And when you follow up, you're strengthening your image.

Here are the basic formulas to follow to help you build your reputation and achieve results through follow-up.

Formula 1

Condition Yourself to Stick to a Follow-up Program

Realize that follow-up requires effort, but that your efforts will pay off in increased results. You will be required to make an investment of your time and to commit yourself fully to the program. The results will be worth it. You'll have to change some habits, but you'll be operating more efficiently and effectively. You'll stay in control of the demands taking place around you. These pointers will speed you on your way:

1. Commit yourself to follow up regularly—every day. Think of follow-up as a daily activity, as necessary as at-

tending a scheduled meeting or checking on supply levels.

2. Set aside time for follow-up; if possible, the same time(s) every day. But whenever you do it, clearly tell yourself that you are following up—it's not just "calling Harry to find out that delivery date." You are following up because a delay could affect your schedule or someone else's schedule and you need to communicate that to others.

3. Group similar follow-up activities together so that you keep your sanity and your schedule in order. Concentrate on accomplishing one group of follow-up activities at a time.

4. Tell yourself that follow-up will pay off. And it will, but you may not have instantaneous results. It may take months before you get that appointment, or you may not know if your letter was received; but doing that bit of follow-up will have delivered the message that you're still there, and you will have made an impression.

Formula 2

Rearrange Your Priorities

If you want to follow up, first determine what keeps you from accomplishing it:

- Too much paperwork
- Too many interruptions
- Bad memory
- No established mechanism for follow-up

These are all valid deterrents to following up, but they all assume some other priority besides using follow-up as a way to increase your effectiveness.

Let's take a look at some typical situations where follow-up techniques could be employed but some other priority intrudes:

Situation 1.   You attend a seminar and come back with information useful to your co-workers; you think about writing a report but your desk is buried under piles of memos to be answered, phone messages to return, problems needing your attention, and people waiting to see you.

Situation 2. You read an article on how to stop smoking and it reminds you of a potential client who is trying to kick the habit; you think about calling him, but the thought has slipped your mind by the end of the day.

Situation 3. You agreed six weeks ago to meet a client's deadline and you've been working furiously on it these last weeks; you're a little behind schedule but you feel comfortable about making the deadline. You haven't spoken to the client since early in the project, and now she calls and asks how you're doing.

In every one of these described situations, follow-up could have been used to your advantage, but there's always some more immediate task that needs to be addressed. But in each situation, you missed the opportunity to win points!

How could follow-up have been used to advantage in these situations?

Situation 1. *Writing a report is overwhelming*
You have more work awaiting your expert attention than you can deal with. So break the task down into more manageable parts—but don't put it off. Think smaller than a full report—obviously, you don't have the time for dedicated organization:

• Send a short memo outlining the highlights of the seminar, and then follow up with the full report at a later date (if you feel that's necessary).

• Call a short meeting and tell your co-workers about the seminar. Give them your highlight list as a memory tool.

• Let them know you attended the seminar; make follow-up a priority equal to getting caught up.

Situation 2.   *Bad memory keeps you from what?—I forget*
                 This is a common situation—some of us win points and others don't even recognize the opportunity to establish a contact and cement a friendship. Aren't you delighted when someone remembers a particular personality quirk of yours or one of your interests; or at least you've made enough of an impression so that someone is reminded of you?

• Clip that article and send it right away.
• Write a short "this reminded me of our discussion" note on it—you'll be putting yourself in that person's mind and creating the impression of having a great memory.

Situation 3.   *Client inquiry about the status of a project*
                 If that client had been informed regularly about the status of the project, she would not be making that panic call and wondering about your capability. Keeping clients informed is a follow-up technique that goes a long way toward enhancing your reputation as an effective person. The moral here is "Get to them before they get to you."

• Mark your calendar at realistic intervals to check up on or pass along information about projects in progress.
• Exchange that information with the necessary parties.

Formula 3

Build up Your Information Files

In order to follow up, you need to collect as much useful information as you can and put it to work for you. Don't rely on your memory—it can fail you just when you need it most.

Many times we receive information and don't know what to do with it. We have no place to store it except in our brains; or worse, it doesn't occur to us to store it. The follow-up program is designed to help you develop the systems you need for your profession. Let's apply systems design techniques in four situations:

Situation 1.   You perform a routine tune-up on a car and inform the owner that the throttle shift on the carburetor is worn and should be replaced; the owner decides to live with it for now.

Situation 2.   You sell an art deco cigarette case to a customer who collects items from that period; you tell the customer to check back with you from time to time because you may find other items of interest on your buying trips.

Situation 3.   You sell a suit and a tie to a customer, but a perfectly coordinating shirt is temporarily out of stock; you tell the customer you're expecting another shipment soon.

Situation 4.   You are responsible for securing public and private sector funds, and you oversee the activities of the people developing the proposals and providing the management expertise described in those proposals. Your work is heavily project-oriented, with an awful lot of information for you to keep track of.

In Situation 1, you have the opportunity to follow up with the car owner to find out how the car is running. Will you remember to call the owner again in two months, six months? Probably not with everything else you have to do. Therefore you need a follow-up system that will tell you to call the car owner again.

Set Up a File Card System by Dates

1. Collect your customer's business card, or make a card with the person's name, address, and phone number.
2. Write the nature of the follow-up to be done:
   Tune-up done 1/10/83
   Should replace throttle shift—check back on 4/10/83
3. Place the card in a monthly file folder under April.
4. Check your file folder regularly and follow up in April— your customer will be impressed!
5. No action to be taken now? Then update the card, change the follow-up date, and move the card to the appropriate month in the file folder.

In Situation 2, you have the opportunity to provide personal service to a captive audience. You'll want a follow-up system that will tell you what your public wants.

Set Up a File Card System by Interest

1. Collect a business card, or make a card with the person's name, address, and phone number.
2. Write the person's interest on it: art deco pieces 2/20/83
3. Make a category or interest card and place the card alphabetically in a card file.
4. Keep adding category or interest cards to your file whenever you learn of one.
5. Check your card file at least weekly.
6. Follow up:
   • Call the person when you have the item.
   • Tell the person you've put the item aside and extend an invitation for viewing it.
   • Send a postcard when you have items someone might be interested in.

This file card system can also work to help you remember people and their interests and to show that you can be thoughtful. This system would be very useful in the earlier-described situation about the nonsmoker. When you remember people, they remember you.

In Situation 3, follow-up is the means to building, maintaining, and expanding your clientele. Follow-up means taking action after your words. It's a communication process, so the key element is, once again, people. If you can personalize the selling experience, you can use that to your and your client's advantage.

Set Up a File Card System by Out-of-Stock Items

1. List each temporarily out-of-stock item on a file card.
2. List the requesting customer's name, address and phone number, and the date requested on the card.
3. Keep adding file cards whenever a requested item is out of stock.
4. Check your card file at least weekly.
5. Follow up:
   - Call the supplier for an expected delivery date.
   - Call the customer with this information.
   - Call the customer when the item arrives.

This situation can bring more results because follow-up presents the opportunity to see a client again, to offer additional service, to expand a sale. Follow-up sets apart the good salespersons from the great ones!

Some of the steps you can take to improve your sales techniques are:

1. *Make Selling an Information Gathering Process*
   Find out about your client's particular likes and dislikes:
   - Why is your client buying this product or service?
   - Is this a replacement, change of product or vendor, or first-time use?
   - Were you recommended, referred by advertising, location, telephone?

2. *Assess Your Client*
   - Does your client have time or price constraints, deadlines?
   - Is your client always looking for a particular item, brand, quality, color, size?
   - Does your client have particular needs or problems?
   - Has the client gained a favorable impression of you and your services?

3. *Assess Your Own Operation*
   Make use of the information you've gathered from your client:
   - Do you need to alter the way you are operating?
   - How can you communicate this information to others in your organization?
   - What can you do to reinforce the positives and eliminate the negatives?
   - How can you use this information to bring more results?

In Situation 4, the large coordinating element of the job can sometimes seem overwhelming. But without systems, opportunities can be lost and deadlines missed—and that means money. You need a system that will help you keep control over the variety of activities.

Set Up a Project File System by Date

This system works best when you provide services that must meet schedules and completion dates. Very often, other services and schedules are contingent upon your meeting the one needed or agreed upon. This particular system may seem elaborate at first but it does have certain advantages: It will allow you to keep track of your projects at all times; it aids in scheduling, because you can see how many projects are overlapping; and it helps you to get in the habit of keeping your clients informed.

1. Obtain a large three-ring looseleaf notebook in a bright color, so you can easily spot it.
2. Insert twenty-four tabbed index dividers in the notebook—you'll use two dividers for each month.
3. Write "January 1–15" on the first divider, "January 16–31" on the second, and so on, for the rest of the year.
4. For each new or in-progress project, take a sheet of looseleaf paper and write the client's name, project purpose, and expected completion schedule on it.
5. Break down each project into the steps to be completed by certain dates. If there is more than one month between any two dates, add an in-between date and write "Follow Up" next to the date. Thus, no more than two or three weeks should pass without your following up on it in some way.
6. Going by the closest upcoming date, place each project sheet in the appropriate half-month section.
7. Review the entire current half-month folder every week.
8. Follow up on each project in the current folder: make phone calls, obtain information, keep the client informed.
9. Revise dates, if necessary, and move the sheet to the next listed date.
10. When the project is completed, move the sheet ahead one month (or to suit yourself or the project). Follow up again on its progress when you're reviewing that half month. Just because the project has been completed, don't think about dropping it—follow up on it.

Now you have your choice of several systems that will make it easier for you to follow up and will get you in the habit of following up. These are some of the ways you can control the information floating around you so you can get started on your follow-up program. Follow-up does require you to make an investment of your time, but when you see that investment come back to you in more sales, more referrals, more positive comments and greater results, it's to your advantage to follow up.

Prepare yourself for follow-up. Take a look at your own operation. Do you follow up regularly? If your answer is no or "I don't have the time for it," then you're in need of some systematized follow-up programs.

Here are some follow-up techniques practiced by people I have met or read about. These are some of the ways they make an impression:

A Dentist. After I've had my teeth cleaned at the dentist, the dental assistant gives me a postcard to address to myself—it's one of those postcards with a silly cartoon on it stating something humorous about "check-up time is here again." The postcard goes into a file folder dated five months ahead and gets mailed to me on schedule so I can call to make an appointment (sometimes I wish my dentist weren't so thorough).

A Cosmetics Salesperson. After buying some cosmetics at a department store, I received a postcard from the salesperson, thanking me for my purchase and hoping I would enjoy the products. Naturally, her name and phone number were written on the card, should there be any need to contact her. And every couple of months since that first time I receive a card telling me about an upcoming promotion or a new product.

A Personnel Assistant. A personnel assistant at a large savings and loan association with six branches has the responsibility for interviewing potential applicants. Usually the request for a position to be filled will come directly from the manager of the particular department. The interviewer has learned that people always want to know how soon the position will be filled, whether anyone decent has applied for it, and why it takes so long to get anything accomplished. So periodically, usually once a week, the interviewer calls the requestor and presents a status report on the vacant position, describing progress made and candidates seen. (This interviewer is definitely a graduate of the "get to them before they get to you" school of business.)

The interviewer engages in some solid preventive medicine through this follow-up technique, and accomplishes a great deal: (1) the requestor knows the interviewer is trying to fill the position and hasn't forgotten about it; (2) the interviewer keeps the requestor informed and free from worry; (3) the interviewer gains a reputation for being competent and reliable.

An Executive Recruiter. Executive recruiters, or head-hunters as they are familiarly known, continuously have to keep aware of the activities of the people they place and the companies they place them in. I recently read about the head of a large executive recruiting firm who sent more than 1,200 Christmas cards to clients and acquaintances, and on each note he wrote a short personal message—now that's dedication to follow-up.

Follow-up can be accomplished in a number of ways. The important point is to do what you said you would do: If you told a client you would call when you received the next shipment of red pullover sweaters size XL, do it; if you said you would find out if the manufacturer is still producing that model, find out and let the client know the results; if you have to change a delivery date, tell the affected parties. In short, always keep people informed and keep your word—do what you said you would do—follow up! Through follow-up you have the chance to create a favorable impression with others. Follow up or fall short—doesn't that make you want to rearrange your priorities right now?

Follow-up Formulas

1. Condition yourself to stick to a follow-up program.
2. Commit yourself to follow up regularly—every day.
3. Set aside time for follow-up, if possible the same time every day.

4. Group similar follow-up activities together so that you keep your sanity and your schedule in order.
5. Tell yourself that follow-up will pay off.
6. Rearrange your priorities; determine what keeps you from following up.
7. Hold the catch-up—break tasks down into manageable parts.
8. Send notes and articles to keep people aware of you.
9. Use a calendar to mark information about projects in progress.
10. Get to them before they get to you.
11. Build up your information files:
    - Set up a file card system by dates.
    - Set up a file card system by interests.
    - Set up a file card system by out-of-stock items.
    - Set up a project file system by dates.

12. Prepare yourself for follow-up; assess your own situation and then follow up.

VII. Job-Related Activities

This is your life!

Now here's a situation where you can really shine like the star you are—preparing for and getting a job.

Many people are terrified at the thought of having to go on an interview or writing a résumé or competing for a job. Me—I love to go on interviews. It gives me the chance to meet new people and form new contacts; to learn about other companies' operations; to sharpen my interviewing skills; to learn what qualities are valuable in today's marketplace; and to validate my feelings of self-worth about my accomplishments.

Everyone thinks a résumé is needed only when job opportunities crop up. Not so. A résumé represents a record of your accomplishments. An up-to-date résumé tells what you have achieved and helps you to evaluate your goals.

A résumé should be part of your personal portfolio, along with some other tools of the trade. Let's examine each of these tools in some detail.

Tools of the Trade

There are a number of ways in which you can proudly record your accomplishments; the means you choose will certainly depend on the position you have now, whether you're trying for full-time or free-lance work, and the kind of impression you're trying to make.

Business Cards

The business card has become a staple item in a person's presentation package:

- It's something to exchange with others at business meetings or chance encounters.
- It gives people a record of your name and line of business.
- It's easy to store in a business card file box.
- It lets people know you're important enough to have a business card.

Now this last point is silly, because anyone can have a business card. If you have any sort of position in which you make outside business contacts, you need a business card. Mention this fact to your boss—you may not be able to get personalized cards with your name imprinted on them, but you should at least be able to have cards stating the company's name and then you can always handwrite your name and telephone number on them.

If you are in business for yourself, even if it's just part-time photography work you do as a hobby, get yourself some business cards. Your potential clients will be able to keep your name on file and call you when a need arises.

If you're in business to stay, then it would be worth your time and money to consult a graphics design person for an attractive business card. You can get quite fancy with different colors of paper and ink, gold foil stamping, engraved lettering; or you can go the simple route with one color ink on good quality paper.

If you're not sure of yourself yet, or can't make a big money investment for design work, fret not—any local printer, even your neighborhood copy center, will be glad to help you design a card.

The standard business card measures 3½" long by 2" wide and usually reads with the printing across the long side; but for a different touch you can turn it on its side and have printing across the width. What's important are the words on the card: your name, address, phone number, and your title or a short description of the service you provide. You might also want to include any information that would make it easier for people to locate you, such as special hours, directions, or home phone number if that's appropriate. Here are two sample business cards:

WALTER GOODMAN
WATCHES • DIAMONDS • JEWELRY
FINE WATCH REPAIRING

170 MAIN STREET
ROOM 314
781–9259   ANYTOWN, NY 12345
ENTER ON ELMWOOD

Special Gifts for Special People
We Cater to Lefties

THE SOUTH PAW SHOP

Open 10:00–5:00   Catalog Sales
341 Broadway   P.O. Box 212
Utopia, CA 90000   Utopia, CA 90001
Closed Monday   (213) 123–4567

I keep a business card file box on top of my desk; whenever I have to locate a card, my trip through the file box usually turns out to be an adventure. I love trying to remember who these people are and where I met them. To aid my memory I have taken to filing cards according to business or service provided rather than by last name. It's much easier for me to find Tom Taylor's name under *L* for *Legal* than to try to remember the name of the law office administrator I met at a legal convention at Caesar's Palace in Las Vegas two years ago. On the back of the card I do write the date and place where we met.

Your business card should serve as a memory aid, to help people remember you and find you. And when you get that first referral from someone looking at your card, you'll be glad you made sure to get them.

Brochures

You already have a business card to leave with business contacts and colleagues; now think about how much more a brochure could do for your business. Not everyone needs to have a personal brochure. If you're in a staff support position at an organization, there's really no reason for you to have a brochure. But if you're in business for yourself, as a consultant, free-lancer, or full-timer, you should think seriously about putting together a brochure that describes your services and background, and maybe has a client list and client comments.

We may forget specific names on business cards, but we always remember brochures. In fact, we probably remember them because so few people have brochures and we're impressed by the people who do. We may discard business cards, but we tend to keep brochures. Psychologically, they seem so much more permanent and important than business cards. And they're so much more complete: The brochure contains a description of the product or service and gives some background information on the qualifications of the provider. So in looking over the brochures someone can make a preliminary determination as to whether this person has the right product and experience for the job in question.

An informative brochure should answer the usual questions people will have about your services (for instance, my brochure gives suggestions for the ideal number of people who could attend my training sessions and the length of time for each seminar), so that when they call you they'll have some general ideas about the way you operate your business. You might want to include prices in your brochure (for the item or your rates); but then you have locked yourself in with those prices and either you couldn't raise them or would have to print new brochures every time you have an increase (writing in new figures over old ones shows a lack of style and is just downright tacky).

There's another advantage to having a brochure: It can be passed around for others to examine—a lot more easily than you can be. This helps in situations where several people are being considered for a service. Your brochure can help illuminate the spoken appraisal; or maybe this person can't use your services but will pass your brochure along to someone who can—that's how to get mileage out of your brochure.

The size of the brochure can vary depending on how much you have to say; but don't overdo it—after all, leave them with something to find out about you.

It should be able to fit into a No. 10 business-size envelope (that's the regulation long one)—you want your brochure to look good, not awkward. Your brochure can be any one of these sizes:

$8\frac{1}{2}'' \times 11''$—folded in three parts

$8\frac{1}{2}'' \times 7\frac{1}{8}''$—folded in half

$8\frac{1}{2}'' \times 7\frac{1}{8}''$—folded in half with additional pages stapled inside.

You'll notice that the brochure is always 8½″ long by 3½″ wide—that's the standard look.

The front page should carry your company name and logo, if you have one, or your personal name; your address and phone number; and a statement about the product or personal service you provide.

The back of the brochure will carry a short résumé or your experience and qualifications; list your education and any honors or awards here as well.

The inside of the brochure is where you spell out the distinguishing features of your work, how you do it, what you do, and a little bit about what makes you special. You can, if you want to, include a list of clients and maybe testimonial comments from some of them.

Break down the ideas on the inside of your brochure into categories—it will be much easier to read and more pleasing to the eye.

This is what my brochure looks like:

PRESENTATIONS WITH IMPACT

By Caryl Winter

Workshops in Business
Communications

- Letter/Report Writing
- Policies/Procedures

Caryl Winter would like to help your company. Here's what she does:

- Works with management to identify specific communications concerns

- Focuses on your needs—studies your systems

- Works with you to identify specific weaknesses and then defines the contents of the workshop and the participants

Here's how she does it:

- Works with small groups to improve their communication skills

- Conducts seminars within your company—in half-day, full-day, or weekly workshops

- Encourages participants to share and solve particular communication problems.

And she wants to do it for your company! Call her to discuss a specialized presentation.

Caryl Winter
400 S. Beverly Drive, Suite 312
Beverly Hills, CA 90212
(213) 933-0933

Workshops in Business Writing and Speaking

Skills Gained

- How to identify your objective

- How to assemble and develop the material for presentation

- How to get organized and stay there

- How to build your case

- How to use visual aids

- How to create and maintain interest

- How to make powerful presentations

- How to take and get ACTION

- The importance of FOLLOW-UP

Workshops in Developing Policies and Procedures

Skills Gained

- How to define policy

- How to identify your objective

- Differences between policies and procedures

- How to write effective procedures

- How to communicate new and revised procedures

- How to develop a policies and procedures manual

Caryl Winter

With 15 years of experience in progressively improved corporate positions, Caryl has taken her enthusiasm, energy, and expertise into the general marketplace. She developed *Presentations With Impact* to fill the corporate need for improving specific business communications skills. Caryl also serves as continuing education instructor for UCLA in the School of Management, Labor, and Business, and teaches seminars in Business Communications, Report Writing, and Résumé Writing.

Caryl's prior experience encompasses these results-oriented activities:

- Internal communications development
- Methods and procedures analysis
- Word processing needs assessment
- Forms design and printed materials management (award-winning concepts)
- Training and development specialist
- Communication tools:
  employee handbooks, procedures manuals, secretarial style guides, house organs, annual reports, brochures.

Caryl received the Master of Arts degree from New York University in English/Communications and the Bachelor of Arts degree in English from American University in Washington, D.C. She has written trainers' guides for use with films on supervisory and training skills, has reviewed textbooks on business communications, and is always involved in understanding and commenting upon group dynamics.

When you make the decision to have a brochure, work with a graphic designer on the layout and look of the information. Ask people you know to make recommendations; shop around until you've found someone you like and can work with; ask to examine examples of their work. A brochure is an investment of your money (it will probably cost a couple of hundred dollars for five hundred brochures); but it's also a reflection of your capabilities, and you do want the best for yourself.

Biographies

No, not your life story; just a short synopsis highlighting the achievements of your professional career.

What's the difference between a bio and a résumé? And who needs one?

A bio presents a summary of your accomplishments. It is written in complete sentences in narrative form, as contrasted with the résumé, which is written in phrases and arranged in chronological sections. The bio refers to you by name within the body of information (Caryl received the master of arts degree in English from New York University); the résumé is cold (Education: master of arts, English, New York University). Here's what a bio looks like:

Karen Riley

Karen is presently a third-year student at St. John's University in Jamaica, New York. Her major field of study is communications, with emphasis in the areas of film production, television production, journalism, radio broadcasting, and public relations.

For the past two years Karen has worked at the Television Center at St. John's. In that time she has learned to operate color and black and white cameras, the audio board, the switcher, the videotape machine, the character generator, and the shader. She is also familiar with basic lighting techniques, specifically key, fill, and back lighting.

The Television Center produces a variety of shows, and two of them have appeared on commercial television. These shows were an Italian-American series on CBS in the summer of 1981 and a Spanish series on ABC's *Listen and Learn*, also in the summer of 1981. A bilingual Spanish/English series has aired on channel 47, and Karen served as technical director on one show and worked the camera on others. A gifted children's program airs regularly on Saturdays, and this show is affiliated with NBC. Other shows are produced for local viewing by the school. Karen has also directed two productions using videotape.

In addition to working at the Television Center, Karen is an officer of the Television Club at St. John's. She instructs other club members in the proper use of the equipment in the Television Center. All club members are encouraged to write and direct productions, and so far the Television Club has had the pleasure of directing and producing a show on cable television recently.

Karen also produced and directed an ITV show on lighting, and has produced and directed other club members' productions.

The bio is handy to have when you know someone would be more comfortable reading a short summary of your background (a bio is usually less than one page) or when information about you is needed for reprinting in a press release, program, or article—in other words, if someone needs information about you to be passed on to another source, send a bio. Send it in a package with your brochure and business card.

Résumés

Brochures and biographies are some of the more exotic tools to add to your personal presentation kit. But absolutely everyone needs a résumé. And that's where the problems begin: If you don't have a résumé and never have written one, if you have one but haven't updated it in years or don't even know if it is an effective one, the task seems overwhelming.

But, if you have incorporated the monthly progress report into your life-style, then you already have the makings of a résumé. Your progress reports are a résumé of your accomplishments; sure, you'll have to condense some material but you'll have a good head start on yourself.

A résumé is not something that you just send out in response to newspaper advertisements or give to people you meet at job fairs. It is your own assessment of your capabilities—be proud of yourself; you deserve it.

A résumé is not a job description, but that's the trap we fall into when writing one. It's easy to describe what you do; but then so will every other person who has your job title, so how can you set yourself apart from them? By using your résumé to show what a valuable person you are; what changes you made; what goals you set and met; and what new systems you designed. That's the difference between a résumé and a job description.

But you say you still don't know how to write one? Let's take it from the top:

1. *Personal Information.* Begin with your first and last name, in capital letters, centered at the top of the page. (Do not use the words *Résumé* or *Summary of Accomplishments*, or, heaven forbid, *Curriculum Vitae*—that would be like putting the word *Letter* at the top of your letter.) Centered under your name, but not in capital letters, place your home

address and home phone number. (Career moves should be handled at home, not at your present place of employment.)

2. *Objective*. This is the area where we separate the adults from the children. Some people will tell you not to put one in—that it's too limiting; others will tell you to tailor your objective to the position you're seeking—but isn't that limiting too? I offer a compromise: State an objective that explains what you can offer to others, rather than the kind of a position you're seeking. For example:

These Objectives Say "Others"	*These Objectives say "Me"*
To contribute to developing results-oriented marketing and advertising skills within a management setting	A challenging position utilizing my marketing and advertising skills, with room for growth and career potential
To be an integral part of a growth-oriented management team, that will utilize my business, tax, and real estate background to facilitate profitable growth	A financial management position in a profit-oriented organization that demands managerial skill and provides appropriate rewards for measured success

The difference between an ordinary objective and an effective one is stating what you can contribute. Spend some time wording your objective. It will be the hardest part to write, but remember, it's the first thing your reader reads.

3. *Education*. An often-asked question is: Should the education section or the experience section be listed first? What's the proper procedure? The order or arrangement is your choice, based on your own situation:

- If you're recently out of school, list your educational background first.
- If a particular degree is essential in your field, list your educational background first.

- If your experience counts more than your education, list your experience first and education after.
- If you have been out of school a while (your age is your business), list your experience first and education after.

If you have a college degree or degrees, list them in reverse chronological order, with the most recent degree first. The order is degree, major area of study, year, school, and location:

> Master of Arts, Communications—1968
> New York University, New York, New York
>
> Bachelor of Arts, English—1968
> American University, Washington, D.C.

If you don't have a college degree yet, but you're working toward one, list the school and major and the expected date of completion. That shows you're goal-oriented:

> Bachelor of Arts, Personnel Administration
> Northridge University, Northridge, California
> Expected completion date: June 1984

If you don't have a degree but you've taken some adult education courses or attended some work-related seminars, list the significant ones:

- Supervisory development program
- Advertising and sales promotion concepts
- Financial planning in the eighties.

4. *Experience*. Your résumé should contain information about your experience that answers these questions:

- What kind of company do you (did you) work for? Unless the company name and prominence are widely known, describe it: "Marketing manager for ABC Consolidated, Inc." is irrelevant to me; but "Marketing manager for an electronics supply company with annual sales of $150 million" is relevant.

- What were your direct responsibilities?
- Were you ever promoted?
- Did you change the nature of your job in any way?
- Did you save your company money in any way?
- Did you help increase sales?
- Did you implement new policies or procedures?
- Did you train or supervise anyone?
- Where do you show that you can work with people?

For example:

Administrative Secretary

Handle secretarial and administrative duties for systems engineering group; duties include complex technical dictation, composing and typing correspondence, and scheduling appointments and meetings; also responsible for department budget, preparing formal documents, and making foreign travel arrangements; exercise independent judgment in performing these duties.

Retail Clerk

Assist in ordering and receiving merchandise for a supermarket with annual sales of $2 million; verify invoices against orders; and inventory supplies.

Controller

Manage the financial responsibilities for five related companies with budgets of $2 million; responsible for accounting and clerical staff of twelve; supervise ongoing activities and preparation of quarterly financial statements, cash-flow projections, and other accounting activities; developed solutions and presentation packages for five companies in order to obtain government and private sector backing.

Manager, Internal Communications

Served as assistant vice-president responsible for writing and disseminating bank policy and procedures to all twenty-five branches; recommended and installed a word processing system to maintain the bank's system of manuals and to improve the timely distribution of revisions; implemented a monthly communications bulletin to inform users of changes and to improve the flow of information; provided ongoing hiring, training, and upgrading of eighteen employees to expand the overall services of the department.

Your experience section should include a picture of the skills that you can contribute. Remember to specify dollars, numbers of people, and exact results—that's what will set you apart.

Your experience section should be your heaviest, and I do mean weight. This is the section that is read with the most interest and the most time—after all, wouldn't you have the greatest interest in someone's experience?

Let me spend a few moments describing the format for the experience section, since you'll probably want to concentrate most of your energy on this section. From the top:

a. List the dates of employment on the left side of the page, and on the same line as the dates, list your company name and general location:

> March 1980–   Associated Airservices, Inc.
> Present   Torrance, California

b. Skip a couple of spaces and state your position title and summary of accomplishments. Underline your position title, and use concrete, active phrases to describe your experience.

c. Continue to cover, in reverse chronological order, the various positions and position descriptions you have filled:

  • Use active phrases and words to describe your accomplishments.
  • Do not write in complete sentences.
  • Do not refer to yourself or use personal pronouns—be brief and succinct.

Active Words to Use in Your Résumé

administered	designed	improved	recruited
analyzed	developed	investigated	resolved
approved	directed	managed	revised
arranged	distributed	moderated	scheduled
conceived	enlarged	negotiated	served
conducted	established	notified	strengthened
contracted	examined	organized	supervised
controlled	expanded	performed	systematized
coordinated	guided	planned	trained
created	implemented	presented	wrote

  • Use semi-colons between phrases(;) and a period at the end of each experience section(.)

d. If you were promoted while working at the same company, be sure to include that:

March 1980–   XYZ Financial Ltd.
Present   St. Louis, Missouri

Controller (promoted March 1981):_____
_____
_____

*Assistant Controller:*_____
_____
_____

5. *Memberships*. List the organizations you are actively involved with, if they are relevent to your career goals.

6. *Honors and Awards*. List the special proud moments in your life, especially if they relate to your career plans. (Winning the Fire Prevention Award in the third grade is wonderful, but is it relevant to your desire to supervise the bookkeeping division of a manufacturer of gloves?)

7. *Military Experience*. If you have been in the reserves or the armed forces, mention it proudly—you earned it.

8. *Personal Stuff*. Not necessary. This kind of information—about your age, health, spouse (if there is one), or children (if they exist, with or without a spouse) or your free-time hobbies—is not relevant to your obtaining a particular position.

9. *References*. State these words, and only these words: "References available upon request." Only when a job has almost been offered and your soon-to-be-boss wants to verify your credentials should you release the names of private individuals who can be contacted—not before. Their names should not be listed on the résumé, nor should you attach recommendation letters. And when you do give someone as a reference, always be sure to get that person's permission and tell them about the possibility of an upcoming reference check.

That's it. These items reflect the standard formats and information to include in preparing a résumé. Here are two samples. One is for a young woman still in college; the other for a man with a great deal of work experience:

KAREN RILEY
168-15 204th Street
Kew Gardens, NY 11364
(212) 268–0149

OBJECTIVE: To assist in all phases of television direction and production.

EDUCATION

Bachelor of Arts in Communications
St. John's University, Jamaica, New York
Expected completion date: June 1983

Major areas of study: Film Production, Television Production, Journalism,
                       Radio Broadcasting, and Public Relations

EXPERIENCE

1980–Present   Television Center
                      St. John's University
                      Jamaica, New York

Equipment Experience

- color and black-and-white cameras
- audio board
- switcher
- videotape machine
- character generator
- shader
- basic lighting, including key, fill, and back lighting

Television Production Experience

- Italian-American series on CBS, summer of 1981
- Spanish series on ABC's *Listen and Learn*, summer of 1981
- various productions for St. John's University:
  —bilingual series on Channel 47 (served as technical director on
    some shows)
  —gifted children's program, affiliated with NBC

Radio Experience

- engineer radio classes:
  —work the audio board
  —monitor voice levels
  —cue records on turntable

MEMBERSHIP

Officer, Television Club, St. John's University

- responsible for teaching members how to use equipment in Television Center
- produced and directed ITV show on lighting
- produced and directed other members' shows

References available upon request.

DENNIS L. JACKSON
1401 Wayne Drive
Los Angeles, CA 90216
(213) 799–0507

OBJECTIVE: To be an integral part of a growth-oriented management team that will utilize my business, tax, and real estate background to facilitate profitable growth.

EXPERIENCE

October 1979 to April 1980   Parks, Adams & Palmer, CPAs
                                    Beverly Hills, California

Staff Accountant: Provided professional tax services for firm's clients; services included tax return preparation, tax research, tax projections; represented clients with IRS, and reviewed work prepared by other staff.

November 1976 to October 1979   Advisers Equity, Inc.
                                       Advisers General
                                           Management Corp.
                                       Stonehedge Group, Inc.
                                       Altech Printing Co.
                                       Associated Airservices, Inc.

Controller: Concurrent controller of five brother/sister companies. Supervised accounting and clerical staff of eight. Responsible for corporate accounting, taxes, cash flows and other related activities. Supplied tax expertise in planning and problem solving of all companies and their partnerships. In charge of monthly financial statements of Universal Heritage Investment Corp., a securities broker-dealer with thirty offices (also a brother/sister company).

July 1976 to November 1979   Westside Community for Independent
                                    Living, Inc.
                                    Los Angeles, California

Executive Director: Implemented initial grant of this nonprofit corporation, a supportive service and counseling agency for the disabled. Acquired office space, set up administrative and accounting systems and procedures, and hired initial staff. Was part of group of seven which envisioned WCIL. Contacted federal, state, and local governmental agencies to provide continuing funding. Obtained IRS and state approval of nonprofit status. Continue to serve as financial consultant.

July 1973 to July 1976   Frye, Coe & Co., CPAs
                                El Segundo, California

Staff Accountant: Prepared and reviewed individual, partnership, corporate, fiduciary and estate tax returns. Represented clients at IRS. Did tax research and answered client inquiries.

October 1968 to July 1973   Mattel, Inc.
                                   Hawthorne, California

Senior Corporate Accountant: From December 1969 to July 1973 assisted director of corporate accounting. Was promoted to staff accountant, then to senior accountant and then to senior corporate accountant. Responsibilities included preparation of SEC reports, financial section of annual report to stockholders, federal and various state income tax returns and other governmental reports. Coordinated annual audit with outside CPAs and tax audits with IRS, Franchise Tax Board, and State Board of Equalization. Prepared consolidated financial statements, projections, cash flows, and other special projects. Coordinated these activities with corporate and subsidiary controllers, vice-presidents, and legal department.

Junior/General Accountant: From October 1968 to December 1969 assigned to general accounting. Started as junior accountant analyzing accounts. Promoted to general accountant. Supervised domestic and foreign consolidations.

LICENSES:	Certified Public Accountant, January 1976
	Real Estate, January 1979
EDUCATION:	Bachelor of Business Administration,
	Major in Accounting
	Kent State University, Kent, Ohio, June 1966
MILITARY:	U.S. Army, September 1966 to September 1968,
	Administrative Specialist.
MEMBERSHIPS:	American Institute of Certified Public Accountants
	California Society of Certified Public Accountants

References available upon request.

One more thing: Don't lie on your résumé; not about the obvious things, such as saying you have a degree when you don't (that fact is too easy to verify), and not about other things, such as saying you wrote the company's annual report when you researched it and wrote a few pages. I know some corporate recruiters will tell you to stretch the truth, to take some liberties with the information. But you're much safer sticking to the facts. If you didn't have full responsibility, don't lie about it. You'll be much happier living up to what you can do rather than what you can't do—spare yourself the anxiety and the ulcer.

Now for the look of your résumé: It should be neat-looking and letter-perfect. That means have it typed by a professional on an office typewriter. Your little home portable and correction fluid just won't do. You may have to have the résumé typed twice, or until you're satisfied with the spacing and layout. Have an expert read over your résumé for proper punctuation and spelling.

Take your résumé to a copy center and have fifty or so copies made on good quality bond paper—the office copier won't do. Use white or ivory paper only; I've seen blue, gray, even orange(!) résumés, but my advice is to stand out in positive ways—not by an unusual looking résumé. And keep your résumé to two pages maximum.

Finally, your résumé should always be up to date; it should always reflect your present job and any recent awards or new associations. Look at it every six months, at the very least, and ask, "Am I still doing these things? What other accomplishments can I add?"

Evaluate yourself and your accomplishments. And do it now.

How to Develop Job-Related Materials

1. Get yourself the necessary tools for your presentation kit:
   - Business cards
   - Brochures
   - Biographical materials

2. Include the necessary information on this material:
   - Name, address, and phone number
   - Description of services
   - Qualifications

3. Develop your résumé right now:
   - Define your career objectives.
   - Include a description of your experience, with the emphasis on results.
   - Stress what you can do.
   - Give people a clear picture of your capabilities.

4. Check your résumé for completeness and correct-
   ness:
   • Verify spelling and punctuation.
   • Make some professional-looking copies.

5. Keep your résumé, and your brochures and busi-
   ness cards, up to date:
   • Ask yourself if you're still doing these activities.
   • Add new accomplishments to the list.

The Interview

How to Conduct an Interview—from Both Sides of the Desk

So your résumé got you in the door. Terrific! But now you're terrified about going on the interview; you're afraid they won't like you and you won't get the job. Well, this is a two-way street you're on—you have to like them and want the job as well!

What do you do when you land the interview? Well, I'll tell you my approach: I regard the interview as a blind date. It could turn out to be the match of my dreams; but if not I will at least have made another career contact, expanded my knowledge base about business, and tried out my interviewing skills. My approach is very similar to the real-world dating game: You wouldn't accept a blind date with just anyone, certainly not before doing some basic checking, so why should you accept a job without doing some research first?

From the Interviewee's Side

1. Find out as much as you can about the company:
   a. Go to the library and read about the company:

- Has the company been in the newspapers?
- Can you get a copy of the annual report?
- Is it a public or privately owned company?

b. Check around with business contacts (remember all those business cards you saved?):
- Is it a known company?
- What kind of reputation does it have within its in dustry?

2. Find out as much as you can about the position:
   - Talk to your contacts.
   - Talk to other people in similar positions.

3. Do your homework before the interview.

Okay, the day of the big date is here:

4. Dress to look your absolute best; dress properly for the occasion:
   - Even if the position will require you to wear a uniform or casual clothes, "dress up" for the interview.
   - Wear a businesslike outfit—a suit for men and a skirt and jacket for women.
   - No matter what type of industry, leave your jeans and t-shirt at home.

5. Arrive on time; better yet, arrive a little early so you can have a look around the office:
   a. Look at the office furnishings:
   - Are people crowded together or do they look comfortable?
   - Are the furnishings modern or do they look like castoffs from a going-out-of-business sale?
   - What kind of office equipment do you see (typewriters, copiers, calculators)—modern or not?
   - Any evidence of plants or artwork?

   b. Look at the people:
   - Do they talk to one another?

- Can they drink coffee at their desks?
- Do they look disgruntled or relaxed?
- Do they have personal items or knickknacks on their desks or around their offices?
- What is the general style of office dress?

6. Smile and look interested and friendly when the interview begins.

The interview will probably begin with a general description of the position and an overview of the company. Then it turns into question time. Remember though, this is a two-way street: You can *ask* as well as answer questions.

7. Answer questions honestly and capably:
- Stress your competency.
- Explain how previous experiences could carry over to these new ones.
- Express your willingness to learn.
- Turn negatives into positives. (If you couldn't get along with your previous supervisor, don't badmouth the person. Express your need for growth rather than their suppression of your talents. If you didn't work for a couple of years, and this is questioned by the interviewer, explain how you spent the time constructively and what you learned from it.)

8. Give as much information as you need to in order to display your competency, but read the interviewer's body language to know when to stop:
- Look for signs of uneasiness or boredom or restlessness.
- Cut your story short—don't prolong it.

9. Ask questions of the interviewer (this is an endless list, but I'll give you some of my favorites):
- What happened to the previous person in this posi-

tion? (Promoted, fired, left the company? Find out where and why.)

- May I talk to that person about the position? (This question really gets them.)
- May I see a copy of the organization chart for this department? Where does it fit within the larger organization? (No organization chart could be a sign of poor management.)
- Does this position have a written job description? Are there written procedures? (Ditto above comment.)
- How do you feel about my becoming a member of _____organization to expand my knowledge? (Job-related, of course; this will give you an indication of whether the company encourages outside learning activities.)
- What are the decision-making channels? (Learn how many layers separate you from the top and what quality of independent decisions you can make.)
- What is the competition for this position, and how do I rate against it? (Get an indication of your chances.)

10. Give them a taste of your insight into how you would handle matters, but just a taste—there's plenty of time to improve matters when you're in the position; anything else is premature and potentially insulting to the people who have lived with the existing system. Take notes during the interview, and then interpret them and offer suggestions.

11. Stress what you can do for them, *not* what they can do for you.

12. When the interview is about to end, ask for a fair appraisal of your qualifications, your presentation, and your chances for the position. Phrase this question as a willingness to improve yourself for another situation, not just as an aggressive desire to know whether you got the job or not.

From the Interviewer's Side

1. Find out as much as you can about the candidate's previous position by talking to your contacts and to other people in similar positions.

2. Be ready to start the interview on time. Set a time limit for ending the interview and stick to it—unless you are so taken with the candidate that you want to continue it.

3. Smile and look interested and friendly when the interview begins.

4. Assess the candidate's nonverbal behavior:
   - Is the person dressed appropriately for an interview and for the general office mode of dress?
   - Does the candidate seem at ease and confident about being in an interview situation?

5. Establish yourself as the manager of the interview:
   - Introduce yourself by name and title.
   - Engage in a bit of friendly banter to put the candidate at ease but also to show you are familiar with the person's background. ("So, I see you're from New York originally, but I'll bet you're glad you're not there this winter.")
   - Get the candidate to loosen up; notice how your opening remarks are accepted. (If the candidate says "Yes" and not another word, then you will have to do a little more loosening-up work or recognize that you may have a nonassertive person on your hands; if the candidate says "Yes, but sometimes I do long for a little snow," you're in business.)

6. Give this person your undivided attention. Leave instructions for no telephone calls to be put through and do not allow any personal interruptions. These interruptions can prolong the length of the interview, break trains of thought, and, worse, damage whatever rapport

you have established. Honor the candidate's time and commit yourself to that.

7. Give a clear picture of the position and the company. Express some bad features along with the positive ones—see how the candidate reacts to these negative features.

8. Find out as much as you can about the candidate, beyond what is stated in the résumé:
   - Ask the candidate to explain some of the activities or responsibilities stated in the résumé. Does the description match the words?
   - Ask questions that illustrate how the candidate gets along with others or works as part of a team.

9. Ask questions that will give you an idea of the candidate's abilities to work, to react to questions and challenges, to think quickly, to communicate, to get along with people.

10. Take notes if you want to, but do tell the person that you are doing so. This can be distracting or threatening to someone if you don't say why you're doing it. ("I just want to jot down some notes to jog my memory.")

11. Answer questions asked of you honestly and capably:
    - If this is a position fraught with problems, or the organization is, let the person know that. (You want to establish your own credibility at the same time you want someone who will be willing enough to accept the position.)
    - Express your willingness to improve conditions, if the candidate raises some issues you know have been neglected.

12. End the interview by giving the candidate a fair appraisal of the situation:
    - If the candidate impresses you as a potential worth-

while employee, someone you would like to talk to again, have other people meet, make sure the person gets the message. ("I'm sure you'll hear from me in a few days. I'd like you to meet_____.")

- If the person has good qualities but you're not sure and want to make an assessment based on other factors, make sure the person gets the message. ("Your background is impressive, but I must be honest with you and tell you that I will be interviewing some others.")
- If the person does not fit the bill, make sure the person gets the message. ("Thank you for taking the time to talk to me. I wish you success in your career development.")

Because job choosing and acceptance can be very much like going on a successful blind date, after the interview you've got to ask yourself some hard questions. And those questions should be examined by both the interviewer and the interviewee:

- Is this someone I want to spend time with?
- Can we learn and grow together?
- Do we have mutual goals and outlooks?
- Does this person fit the bill?
- Will we have fun too?

How to Follow Up—from Both Sides of the Desk

The interview is over, but there are a few follow-up activities you should engage in to help you keep on top of your search.

From the Interviewee's Side

1. Complete an index card for every potential employer you talk to. Include this information:

- Name, address, and phone number of company
- Name of person you interviewed with
- Summary of the interview
- History of action (dates of letters, phone calls, interviews)

2. Write a thank-you note:
   - It can be brief.
   - It should be honest.
   - It should express your continued interest in the company and the position.
   - It should make some personal reference to something you and the interviewer discussed.

3. Write a thank-you note right away—within a day of your interview—to show that you're serious. (See the sample of a personalized thank-you letter that follows.)

4. Wait a week, or as long as you can hold out. Follow up with a phone call. Read the signals: If you don't get a positive response from the phone call within two days, don't waste any more time or effort on this position. (Always maintain your integrity—that's more important than a company that can't make up its mind.)

5. Pick yourself up, dust yourself off, and start all over again.

6. If you do connect with the job you wanted, remember the others:
   - Send thank-you notes to the other companies you have been talking to.
   - Express your gratitude and keep your options open— one never knows what the future has in store.

February 8, 1982

Ms. Phyllis Linsley
Global Advertising Concepts

423 Madison Avenue
New York, New York 10017

Dear Phyllis:

I couldn't help but smile when Paul mentioned that height was not a requirement for a traffic assistant. Though I may not be able to reach everything on my toes, I've never had any difficulty obtaining what I needed.

Your interview with me yesterday was both enjoyable and informative. Learning about how rapidly your company has grown really excited me. I'm anxious to begin my career in advertising with an agency that can offer varied opportunities in the future for me. Since the traffic department is quite small I'm sure my diverse abilities and enthusiasm will be able to shine for the benefit of everyone.

I really appreciate your taking the time and interest to interview me. I'm looking forward to accepting the challenging position of traffic assistant.

Thank you,

Melinda Crawford

From the Interviewer's Side

1. Check references:
   - Call the candidate's most recent employers, if that is acceptable to the candidate. (Don't check with anyone unless you have the candidate's permission.)
   - Explain the position the candidate has applied for and any special qualifications the job requires.
   - Ask for a candid evaluation.
   - Ask for a description of the candidate's work habits— including best and worst traits.

2. Call references—don't write. People will be more candid on the telephone—after all, there's no written record

of evaluations so who could produce the evidence?
- Ask the first reference for the name of another reference, someone who has worked closely with the candidate, and talk to the second reference.

3. Go with your gut instincts. If you have any qualms about the candidate (dirty fingernails may mean sloppiness; evading questions may mean untrustworthiness; no take-charge qualities may mean indecisiveness), think again.

4. Offer the position to the right person.

And to both parties: If a mistake is made, correct it soon—there's no harm in that. But there is harm in continuing in a less than ideal marriage.

How to Interview

1. Approach the situation as you would a blind date: Find out as much as you can about the candidate or the company and the position; go to the library and/or check with business contacts.
2. Dress appropriately for the occasion and the industry.
3. Be on time and give the interview your undivided attention.
4. Smile and look interested and friendly when the interview begins.
5. Answer questions honestly and capably.
6. Present information that displays your competency.
7. Ask appropriate questions—interviewing is a two-way street.
8. Stress your willingness to perform, to accomplish, to learn.

9. Offer a fair appraisal of the interview. Time is too valuable to waste.
10. Follow up by checking references or sending letters.

VIII. Dressing For Impact

How to look like the star you are!

I have a confession to make: When I thought about writing this section, I began to collect all the information that came my way regarding appropriate business dress. I collected newspaper articles published across the United States; I read books; I talked with people in high positions; I talked with people in low positions; I gathered facts and opinions; I evaluated my own opinions.

I concluded that there is no one outfit that will guarantee your success. Nor are there right or wrong colors. Personally, I've worn pink and yellow and brown, and even flower prints, which some people might regard as feminine and nonauthoritative colors, and made out just fine; but I've also worn navy blue and black and gray, regarded as authoritative colors, and I've lost—so what am I (or we) to conclude?

Choose the Style That Is Right for You

You know who you are—live up to it and don't forget it! Be as feminine or as masculine as you want to be—as long as you look as if you're dressed to do business, fit into the situation, and feel comfortable.

For instance, I am a short person (five feet in my bare feet) and have always dressed for my size: I stay away from lots of material, big collars, puffed sleeves, and baggy clothes; because I'm small I look lost in anything but slim-fitting clothes.

I have always dressed for my public: I wear skirts, blouses, and jackets or sweaters. I wear dresses, but I prefer to wear skirt and blouse combinations because I get more mileage from them. I do not wear pants or pant suits because they don't seem businesslike to the people I come in contact with.

I have always dressed for myself: I will not wear "sensible pumps." I have always worn ankle-strap or open-toed shoes—I like the way they look, they are the most comfortable shoes for me, and I will continue to wear them as long as I and my legs are able; I do not wear matching skirted suits, because I find them too rigid for my tastes, and I do not wear blouses with bows to simulate the man's suit and tie look.

So much for my "successful dress" look. I guess I do break some of the so-called rules, but I always dress tastefully, conservatively, and as if I mean business when I come to work. That means I stay away from boots, jeans, clunky noisy jewelry, colored or patterned stockings, low-cut necklines, jump suits, gauze or peasant-look clothes, knickers, and other sportswear items. But that's just it—these items are for sport and play, and don't belong in the office.

Men are lucky—suits, shirts, and ties are here to stay, and they can never go wrong as long as they wear "work" clothes. But women, how they can stray! They can follow fashion dictates and wear knickers, miniskirts, and big tops to the office when they're so much more appropriate for weekend and casual activities.

So we need to return to the concept of two separate wardrobes: work clothes and play clothes. This may be the era of "anything goes" but that's not true in the office environment. What you wear to work may not upset the smooth running of office operations, but it can affect your attitude about yourself. Dress for impact, not to cause a stir about the way you look. If your company has a written dress code, follow it. Most companies will have a vaguely phrased one ("dress in an appropriate manner") or an unwritten one— managers can tell you what they don't want to see rather than what is permissible. If there's no dress code, dress the way the majority of the managers dress.

The way you dress can affect relationships with co-workers and certainly reflects on the image of the company overall. If you have any dealings with the public, remember that you are a representative of that company and your manner of dress speaks for it. The clothes you wear should not reflect negatively on your abilities. Right or wrong, pleasant or not, we can have a value judgment placed on us by others because of the clothes we wear.

Again, let your clothes speak out for your competency. If you mean business, then dress that way.

What to Wear for All Work-Related Occasions

Women

Stay away from tight clothes, low-cut necklines, see-through tops, athletic or sport shoes, lots of jewelry, jeans, and T-shirts.

Do wear comfortable clothes: blouses and skirts, dresses,

jackets, and over-sweaters. Remember that you have to work in your clothes and interact with other professionals.

Resist fads—they'll only be a waste of your money, something you'll wear for one season. If you can afford to buy throwaway clothes each year, good for you; but be aware when you're buying it that it's for a short-term investment. Nothing looks deader than last season's style this season. It's obvious to you and anyone else who follows fashion.

Certain fabrics hold up better than others. I'll take silk, wool, and cotton any day over polyester and nylon. I noticed about two years ago that linen was all the rage—linen suits, linen jackets, linen blouses—but I resisted. You know why? Because some years ago I had bought a linen dress (my first and only) and found out how linen wrinkles the first time I wore it. Boy, does it wrinkle! Every time I stood up I could count the new wrinkles—I wanted to throw myself onto an ironing board. I have never worn any linen fabric since that time, but had a good private chuckle during its recent rumpled resurgence.

Men

You have fewer wardrobe choices, but consider yourself fortunate for that. You'll always look as if you mean business in a dark solid-colored suit, contrasting light-colored shirt, and a tie. The white shirt is still standard for men, but light blue and pale beige are gaining more acceptance; dark shirt colors, although attractive, are best left for wear with sports jackets. And sport jackets for businessmen are still not as acceptable as the standard two-piece suit—navy blue and gray shadings, pinstriped or solid, are your best bets.

I personally can't understand what would make a man buy a black suit and wear it to work. One day I noticed that three men in my department were wearing black suits; I felt as if I had stepped into a mortuary by mistake! And while you're staying away from black suits, stay away from plaid ones as well. The trouble is very few plaids look good over so much material. A plaid jacket is one thing, but plaid pants look better in bright sunlight on the golf course than they do under fluorescent lights in the office.

A private little hobby of mine is to count the number of attractive plaid suits I see. I've been doing this for years and have seen only two, both worn by the actor Gene Barry on his long-ago television show. Recently I thought I would be able to add number three: I saw a man wearing an absolutely smashing plaid suit (the suit wouldn't sound so hot if I described the individual colors, but take my word for it), but as he turned to face me and I got a good look at the hideous tie he had chosen to wear with it, I went back to the count of two.

Dress for Business Trips

If you travel for business, take clothes that will look good after excessive plane and car travel. You may be on the road, but you needn't look as if you've been run over. Fold your clothes before putting them in your suitcase; take them out and hang them up when you reach your destination to get rid of any wrinkles. (A travel iron is a luxury of space we usually can't afford and don't really have time for; try hanging wrinkled clothes in the bathroom when you take a shower—this technique can work wonders.) Take clothes that match with each other: If your tie or skirt only matches one jacket, you're wasting precious suitcase space. Wear your jacket, but take an extra one that coordinates with your pants or skirt. Take along a sweater for warmth—wear it over a skirt or shirt and you'll look more casual, if necessary. Subscribe to the shirt-a-day theory—you might not have the time or energy or the cleaning facilities for fresh laundry. Take clothes that won't show spots so noticeably should you have an accident. And remember, wherever you go you can always buy a replacement if necessary—shopping is a worldwide activity.

Speaking of shopping, buy clothes from someone whose
style you admire. Look at the sales help. Pick out someone
whose dress reflects your particular taste and have that person make suggestions. But always look for and buy quality.
I choose clothes the way I choose people—I want things
that last and that will hold up under time and wear.

Dress for Your Industry

I have a friend who works in the entertainment industry.
Whenever I visit her on the studio lot I take notice of her
outfit: jeans, T-shirts (often bearing funny slogans or some
show advertisement), sandals, casual shirts—not exactly
my idea of office attire. And then I notice that everyone
else on the lot is dressed that way. She would be as out of
place on the studio lot wearing a skirted suit and carrying
a briefcase as I would be wearing her clothes in my line of
business.

Casual clothes are right for the entertainment industry
here in California, and no one thinks you're less than competent for coming to work in jeans and an open-necked
sports shirt.

I have another friend, a management consultant, who
wears only a solid navy blue suit, white shirt, and navy and
white pin-dot tie every time he calls on clients. Every time.
This is his authoritative look, and his clients know he means
business when he walks through the door.

I can tell when my husband is attending his board meeting
or going to see someone at corporate headquarters because
he always wears his navy or gray pinstripe suit with the
vest—his clothes say that this is serious stuff.

And another man, the vice-president of sales for the
western United States of a major food conglomerate, wears
one steady outfit: a long-sleeved v-neck cashmere sweater,
sports shirt, and slacks (he has the most extensive one-style

cashmere sweater collection I've ever seen, and recently got two new colors for Christmas). That's all he wears—in his office, meeting clients, speaking at sales conferences, everywhere. For evening meetings, he wears a sports jacket over his sweater and slacks; sometimes he adds a tie. Has his dress style hindered his career or his advancement? Not a bit.

Remember:
1. Dress for comfort.
2. Dress for your style of business.
3. Dress for your industry.
4. Dress for the occasion.
5. But always dress for yourself.

Clearly there are no strict rules about business dress. You should dress appropriately for your industry—but you should also dress for yourself.

How to Dress for Impact

1. Dress to reflect the competent person you are.
2. Dress to look as if you mean business.
3. Resist fads in styles, clothes, and fabrics.
4. Dress to make an impression, not to cause a stir about the way you look.
5. Follow your company's dress code; or follow your company's leaders.
6. Be aware that you are representing your company through your style of dress.
7. Wear fabrics that travel well and won't make you look rumpled.
8. Buy clothes from someone whose style you admire.
9. Look for and buy quality.
10. Choose clothes the way you choose people—for durability and dependability.
11. Dress for comfort.

12. Dress for your business.
13. Dress for the occasion.
14. Dress for yourself.

IX. Presentation Techniques of the Stars—Case Studies and Testimonials

Here's how I learned to make an impact!

By now you should have a pretty good idea of the variety of presentation methods and when and why to use them. In this chapter, I'd like to introduce you to some people I know and explain how they have incorporated these techniques into their own business situations. Maybe some of their "tricks of the trade" will work for you.

Letters—Small-Business Owner

Ask the person who has to write collection letters how he feels about this task and you're sure to hear moans and complaints. Getting money out of people is just not an easy thing to do. A big headache for the owner of a small business (actually for all of us as well) is cash flow: more going out than coming in.

Ron is the owner of a small graphics design shop. His clients prefer to be billed monthly rather than paying by the job. That's what they say, but collecting is another matter. Ron tried the usual—the standard "please pay me" letters, phone calls, a little stronger letter—but wasn't getting terrific results. So he figured he'd try a humorous approach; after all, the straightforward one wasn't working, so how much worse off could it get? This is the letter he sent to his clients:

Dear——————————————————————:

Spring is in the air: The Dodgers are back in their training camp, shaping up to defend their world championship.

We haven't seen our first robin yet, but your anticipated check would be just the regenerating touch of green that we need. Won't you send us your check right away?

Cordially,

Ron Reiss
Reiss Graphics

Your Account Status as of February 28, 1983

Days Old	
30–45	
46–60	$138.50
61–90	
over 90	62.95
Total Past Due	$201.45

His clients got the message in a humorous but effective way. The last time I saw Ron, he was very pleased with the results of the letter and plans to continue this approach instead of the usual boring hard sell.

Reports—Free-lance Consultant

When I began writing this book, I contacted an ex-secretary of mine to do my typing. For the past two years, Dee has been working as a free-lance word processing operator, handling overload typing on sophisticated machinery.

When I contacted her, Dee was working full time in a law office. One day when we got together to exchange the next batch of book pages for processing, Dee told me she was learning a lot just from reading the draft; she especially liked the section on progress reports. So we talked about how she could incorporate their use into her own situation.

Dee prepared a report listing the number of pages she typed; the number of wills, probate documents, briefs, and court records she processed; and a breakdown of the other miscellaneous duties she was performing. She also made some suggestions about work flow and procedures, based on her own observations and experiences at other legal firms. Was her "boss" impressed! She thanked Dee for making her aware of these procedures and told her to make the valuable changes; she also had no idea of just how much paper was processed around the office and was startled and pleased by the figures. Dee was rewarded with a little extra something for her initiative. Dee says she will continue to prepare these reports for her clients' benefit, but they're to her benefit as well.

Oral Presentations—Hospital Administrator

Bob was appointed as the administrator for a hospital recently acquired by a parent hospital management company.

The hospital, when acquired, was hardly a money maker, but Bob worked steadily and diligently to refurbish the facilities, acquire modern equipment, sell doctors on the hospital's services, expand the staff, and increase the patient load. And after just a few short months, positive progress had been made.

As was customary with all newly acquired hospitals, Bob was requested to discuss his progress and defend his problems before the corporate powers. Bob had attended some of these show-and-tell sessions given by other administrators—b-o-r-i-n-g. So he knew what he wouldn't do: inundate them with statistics, financial comparisons, and a lot of talk.

And he knew what he would do: present an informative slide show, with a touch of irreverent humor to it. For example, his first slide was a picture of a run-down shack in the middle of the desert; that was followed by a picture of the hospital after its facelift (the then-and-now concept). Another slide showed a group of old men seated around a potbellied stove (the medical staff then), followed by a picture of an audience at Carnegie Hall (the medical staff now). And on it went with serious slides of the patient rooms, new laboratories, census development records, new equipment (including our friendly administrator stretched out on the X-ray table), and other information. The last slides showed an old man leaving the run-down shack in the desert (the ex-administrator) and then a picture of you-know-who in his office.

The show ended with applause. Applause! And as the president left the room, he thanked Bob for not boring him with another usual display of facts. Bob had certainly made an impact.

Telephones—Travel Agent

Martha is a travel agent and has been involved in the travel business for over ten years. She prides herself on providing specialized and competent service to her clients. Hers is a business based on repeat business and personal referrals. She can't afford to give her clients less than the best.

Most travel agents will provide you with good service before the trip, but Martha sets herself apart in the interest she shows after the trip. Martha keeps a file card on each trip she plans and notes the party's return date on her calendar (she says she'd be lost without her calendar). When a party has returned from a trip, Martha calls the party to welcome them back and to inquire about the accommodations, food, flight, sightseeing activities, and their general impressions of the trip.

The phone calls take a few minutes of Martha's time, but they're worth the effort. Here's what Martha accomplishes with each call:

- She shows her interest in her clients—that she cares enough about them and their trip to want to find out about them.
- She builds client rapport.
- She adds to her own knowledge of a particular area, hotel, airline, etc.
- She uses that knowledge to reassess future recommendations to other clients.
- She tells her clients what she will do, based upon their evaluations.

All of this information is noted on the client's card so that Martha has a built-in reference file. Some travel agents will argue that these phone calls take too much time; they need the time for developing new business. But Martha's philosophy is sound: Keep the clients you have happy and you'll get return business. Now doesn't Martha sound like the kind of travel agent you wish you had, and wouldn't you recommend her to your associates?

Follow-Up—Real Estate Agent

Lita entered the real estate market at a favorable time: housing prices and interest rates were reasonable. But the state of the economy has changed all that, and Lita finds herself in a depressed yet highly competitive market. How does she excel? By paying attention to each client's specific needs and following up on those details.

Lita always looks at a property before the client has seen it—to familiarize herself with the details, to be able to play up the good points and minimize the less attractive features, and to convey the impression that she knows her business.

Selling a house is no easy task, and Lita doesn't expect to do it on the first outing. That's why she keeps her clients informed of houses in their desired price range, location, and life-style; calls them with new information about prospective properties; and offers to work with them to find the right match.

And when the right match is found Lita doesn't just come to a stop. She continues to follow up, to maintain friendly contact with the satisfied sellers and buyers. She sends gifts when escrow closes: perhaps a plant, outdoor house address numbers, a portrait of the children, or something else that would please the particular clients. And Lita's clients remember and love the personalized service, the detailed follow-up. They remember her when the next sale is necessary, and they refer their friends to her.

Brochures—Hair Stylist

I guess I never thought about hair stylists and what they do to improve their business—other than the usual methods, such as newspaper and magazine advertising, weekly specials, that kind of stuff. But I'm impressed with Toni and the systems she has developed for expanding her clientele.

Toni showed me a brochure she was developing, to use in a direct-mail campaign and as a giveaway item. Before designing the brochure, she had taken a survey of customers, associates, friends, acquaintances, and strangers. It was a multiple-choice questionnaire, asking what you want in a haircut. The result, the overwhelming favorite request, is what she used as the wording on her brochure.

Toni kept a record of how many brochures were distributed and how many customers she got as a result of the brochure. She did the same thing with a flyer handed out on the four street corners near her shop. She recorded the number of new customers and then the new ones who became repeat ones.

Toni tries to make at least two suggestions to each customer. She records this on her "number of suggestions" chart and correlates this information with her gross sales chart. And, not surprisingly, the higher the number of suggestions, the higher her sales. Toni also keeps a record of how often a customer visits her, and sends a "time for your haircut" reminder at the appropriate time.

All of these techniques have helped Toni become a better businessperson and a more effective reader of what her public wants. That's a communicator!

Dress—Stockbroker

Norma is now president of her own securities investment firm and began her career in the financial field at a time when very few women were in it. In fact, Norma was one of the first women to be admitted to the floor of the New York Stock Exchange.

When Norma started out, she had no money, no clients, no nothing—just sheer will to know that this was the field she wanted to make her mark in and was capable of doing so, if only someone would listen to her.

The first thing she did was to go to the bank and take out a personal loan for $1,500. With her $1,500 she splurged on two beautiful and costly outfits—one was a knockout, with real fur around the collar and cuffs of the jacket and around the bottom of the skirt; the other outfit was equally impressive. And she bought hats to match her new outfits. Everyone thought she was nuts—spending $1,500 on extravagant clothes and eating peanut butter sandwiches.

Norma told me that $1,500 loan for clothes was the best investment she ever made. When she showed up for her first appointment, she knocked 'em dead: "She must be successful—how else could she afford to dress that way?" They figured she must know her business. So Norma created an aura of success for herself and garnered many clients in the process (naturally, she was good; you don't make it on fur outfits alone).

Norma added one other touch to her dress presentation: She always wore a hat. Whenever she went to see new or prospective clients, she wore a hat. Pretty soon she became known as "You know Norma—the one with the hat." People knew when she was coming, when she was leaving, and she was easy to spot. Her hat became a noticeable feature, along with her fur-trimmed suit.

Norma used clothes to make a statement about herself, and she didn't have to eat peanut butter sandwiches for very long.

Combination of Techniques— Sales Representative

Just about everything Matt does is impressive. Here's a sampling of his presentation methods.

Matt made a recent career change—from advertising account executive to sales representative for a business journal. He loves his new work and doesn't regret the career change.

Matt calls on prospective new clients and on his existing ones. His usual procedure is to call a client and set up a meeting time. This is confirmed in a letter that specifies the meeting date. While making the first presentation, he prepares for the next one: He knows what his client needs and can picture the more applicable information he can return with the next time. Matt says, "Always prepare for the second call. Don't show everything the first time. Save the more applicable stuff to give you a reason to return."

After a couple of calls, Matt tries to schedule a lunch with the client, so they can get to know each other on more than a business level and in a relaxed way. He keeps a running list of people to call and second-call after a few weeks.

Matt works from a large calendar, noting all his calls, meetings, presentations, and follow-up items. He has a full-size yearly calendar on one wall of his office and keeps a photocopy in his desk. He plans on the photocopy and adds permanent information to the wall calendar. Thus he always is aware of his yearly goals and how he is meeting them.

I was especially intrigued by his filing system. Binders are color-coded according to work in progress, work completed, work requiring follow-up. He has found that he works better with files organized according to categories rather than by the individual names; everything is cross-referenced in easy-to-find locations.

Matt keeps a "did good" file for himself; it contains complimentary notes, pat-on-the-back letters, things of that nature. He uses it to remind him of what he's doing right, and reviews the contents with his secretary. The "did good" file is a wonderful ego builder, especially if things aren't going so good. But with Matt's systematized techniques, I don't think he has to worry about that.

These are just some of the ways in which people I know express their presentation skills. They worked for them—maybe they can work for you.

X. How to Develop Your Own Presentation Program

Go for it!

You've read all about presentation methods and you've seen how some people put them to work in their own situations. What are you going to do for yourself?

Figuring Your Own Needs

Ask yourself what kind of person you are: Do you usually reach for the phone instead of sitting down to write a memo? Or are you the kind of person who says, "I don't want to deal with them; I don't want to talk to them. If I do, more things will happen," so you probably tend to write more than talk.

Do you get responses to your requests? Maybe you need to take a more subjective look at your communication style.

Do you follow up or do you look at those activities as more unnecessary work? If so, perhaps you're not as productive as you could be.

Do you have the tools for promoting yourself as a business person? Do you need business cards? Is it time to revise your brochure? Isn't it about time you wrote a résumé?

Do you get positive comments about the way you dress or do you get negative ones? If you don't get any, maybe a wardrobe overhaul is in store for you.

Do you plan activities properly or are you always in a catch-up mode? Does all the world around you seem organized while you're falling apart? Maybe you need some systems to help you organize your day.

Are you late for meetings? Do you hate to attend them and pray that no one asks you for an opinion? Maybe you're getting a reputation for being the silent one when you're really not like that at all.

Do you plan strategy first or do you just jump in and start writing and talking? Do you get good comments on your presentations or do they usually run to "I don't know what this means?" Maybe you need to spend some more time on your preparation and delivery style.

Are you getting the picture?

Deciding Which Presentation Techniques Work for You

Try them all. Then eliminate the methods that don't work for you or for your situation. Maybe yours is a casual company and people rarely write reports; or maybe it's the other way around. You have the right to pick and discard presentation methods, based on your own skills and your work environment. Ask for comments from people. Tell them what you're trying to do and ask for constructive criticism— then improve your techniques.

Sometimes there are time factors: If you need an answer right away, call; don't lose two or three days in the mail. But if you want some practice in improving your writing skills, test them on a thank-you letter or something that doesn't have a life-or-death cloud over it.

Taking the Plunge

Tell yourself you can do it! If you've never spoken to a group before, organize an informal meeting of two or three friendly supportive colleagues and tell a story. Ask them to comment on your delivery.

If you don't have any systems, develop them. Think in small steps so matters won't seem so overwhelming to you. Break the job down into small manageable tasks.

Make an honest evaluation of yourself. Weigh your strengths and weaknesses.

Modify your presentation methods to suit your style and your time. Keep perfecting your techniques until you're satisfied with your progress.

Go for it and watch the results!

Displaying Your New Presentation Skills

Get out of your vacuum and tell people what you're doing. Write letters and memos describing your activities, if you usually call; or call people, if you usually write.

Start dictating, if you've never done it before, and let people know what a time-saver it is.

Build up your reputation for reliability. Let people know they can count on you because you follow up. Take care of situations before they become problems.

For most of us, our work is an important part of our life. It may be because of the long hours we put in, or the money we earn, or the satisfaction of doing a job well, or our dedication to a cause, a service, a company, a goal. Whatever the reason, our time at work is precious. When you present yourself with impact, that time is not wasted.

So go for it—present yourself right now!

XI. Answers to the Most Often Asked Questions About Presenting Yourself with Impact

And you think "Dear Abby" has problems!

How do I know when to write or call? Or should I do both?

The telephone is an informal method of communication. Use the telephone in instances when speed and informality count. If you need to convey information quickly, use the telephone—and certainly when time is a factor.

But the phone call doesn't allow for documentation. There's no record of what was said and what agreements were reached.

Writing is a more formal communication method. Its drawbacks are time lags (from the time you write the document to the time the reader receives it and can respond to it) and lack of two-way conversation.

But writing provides the documentation you may need, and it shows your organizational and thinking abilities.

Confused? If speed is a factor or the matter is a simple one to resolve, use the telephone. If you want to make a special impact, use the written word. And when you want to confirm oral agreements, do both.

My boss reviews my memo (letter or report) before it goes out and always changes something. How do I handle this situation?

You are not alone in this predicament. I hear this complaint more than any other. It is devastating to be criticized about your writing ability. I'm convinced there's a certain chemistry that takes place when someone reads another person's writing. They involuntarily reach for a pen and just have to put a mark on the paper, even if it's just changing one word, such as *sent* to *forwarded*. Now I ask you, is there a reasonable difference between the two words, enough to justify the word change? Of course not.

What I suggest to you is this: Sit down with your boss and say, "I appreciate your advice and I'm willing to make the suggested changes, but would you explain to me why this word is better, or why this sentence should be eliminated and this paragraph rearranged? Could you show me so I won't run into this situation again?"

Aha! That approach requires a confrontation. Some of us would rather slink back to our desks and redo the letter rather than confront the enemy. But if you don't meet the situation, it will continue.

You might even try an honest approach. If you're gutsy enough you might try this: "I know I'm not a great writer but I think I'm pretty passable, and I'm bothered by my words being changed. If you give me a good reason why this word is better than that word, I'll be willing to accept and learn from the change."

There are times, though, when you are just going to have to say, "My boss is going to make changes, no matter how I say it." And learn to live with that. Ask yourself if it's really such a terrible thing or if you can adjust to it. It is time-consuming, but sometimes it's inevitable. There are people in this world who feel compelled to change something on everything they read.

I have to write at least three or four drafts of a memo before sending it out—and I still don't think it's perfect. How can I get it right the first time?

You probably never will. It sounds as if you're never satisfied. So realize that you'll never be perfect and ask yourself if your energy should be directed at rewriting this document three or four times. Couldn't your time and expertise be put to some better use?

Writing is the only occupation I know where we are taught to think about doing it as a first draft and then doing it over—it has its own built-in failure mechanism. I find this unacceptable. Plan carefully what you want to accomplish before you start to write, and then write it once. Your second run-through should be to correct punctuation and make some minimal word changes.

If your memo makes its point, shows your responsibility, and presents an action ending, let it go. And put your energies someplace else before you drive yourself nuts. Reach the point where you can say, "This is okay; not terrific, but it accomplishes my purpose for writing."

Where do I place charts and graphs in a report—in the appendix, within the body, on separate pages?

If your charts are easy to understand and illustrate the point you just made, put them in the body—right after their mention. If your charts are not essential to the point just made, if they serve as backup, then put them in the appendix as supplementary material.

Try to get all of the chart on the page of your description. If you break a chart, you break continuity for the reader. If it won't fit on the same page, then carry the entire chart over to the next page. In other words, keep your chart together.

How do I condense a half hour's heated discussion into acceptable, readable minutes from a meeting?

It is not prudent to mention that the discussion was heated.

Concentrate on getting down the objectives and issues, not the tangential information. Cite the major accomplishments of the discussion and any decisions reached and action to be carried out. Avoid the "he said that . . ." and "then she replied . . ." syndrome.

All that is necessary in minutes is a summary of the discussion and action: "Tom Hennessey and Carol Burke discussed the necessity of rearranging the offices and furniture." Only those present knew they were ready to throw chairs.

Sometimes when I'm formally speaking to a group, I notice that people are talking to each other. How do I handle that?

Why handle it? Consider yourself a dynamic speaker— you're motivating people to discuss your ideas.

Now if the talkers are disturbing others or the comments are getting out of hand, we're facing another situation. If the talkers are disturbing others, ask them politely to keep it down. One verbal mention is usually enough. If you have an old-fashioned heckler on your hands, well, you're in for some hard times. Try these approaches, each one succeeding the previous failed attempt:

1. Do not respond—no matter how funny or right the comment (that only reinforces the heckler, who has a strong need for approval).
2. If the heckling continues, ask the person to keep it down— politely.
3. Ask a little less politely.
4. Ask the heckler to leave the room. Remember, you're in control; you have the right.

After working with so many groups, I have built-in radar for spotting the heckler. The person always surfaces early, to test my durability. This past semester I thought I was really in for a hard time, especially after I told him no one likes a wise guy. But luck was with me: He never showed up again, and the rest of the group was equally delighted.

Should I return every telephone call I receive?

Yes.

What do I do when someone doesn't return my calls?

First deal with your paranoia and get it under control. Give the person a reasonable period of time in which to answer your call; then decide what to do:

1. If you decide to place another call, leave a more complete message than your name and phone number—state the purpose of the call.
2. Write something instead of calling.
3. Talk to someone else if you can.
4. Drop the matter—sometimes it's better this way.

How do I address a letter to someone when I don't know if the person is a man or a woman?

Some names are confusing. If someone signs a letter "Leslie Malone," do you write "Dear Ms. Malone" or "Dear Mr. Malone"? Why not "Dear Leslie," since they're making your task more difficult?

It is acceptable to address the person by first and last name, as in "Dear Leslie Malone," but why not simplify it to "Dear Leslie"?

If you don't know the person and don't feel comfortable writing to him/her with a first name, that's perfectly understandable. And what about the letter signed "L. Patrick"? Those kill me! Should I write to "Dear L. Patrick"? That seems silly. And I don't like "To Whom It May Concern"—that's much too formal. So I suggest one of two things: Address it to "Dear Reader" or omit the salutation—from the inside address go right to the body of the letter.

I'd love to practice the techniques recommended in this book, but my boss says it's not the "company style." What can I do?

My advice is the same as I gave for the boss who keeps changing words:

1. Find out why. Are the objections valid or a matter of personal preference?
2. Do it in small ways for practice and to keep from getting rusty. Do whatever it takes to keep friendly work relationships, but develop your skills at the same time.
3. Store your techniques in an easy-access brain file and use them when you take a new job.

Exactly how should I prepare for a job interview? The last time I was interviewed was about five years ago and I'm scared.

Get ready for all the fun, mystery, excitement, and intrigue of a blind date. Do a little advance planning to find out what you're getting yourself into, and then plan on having a good time. Put your best foot forward: Remember, you have to like them as much as you want them to like you. Look your best, sound your best. Show interest, but create interest as well—you are a desirable commodity, you know; why else would you be wanted for this interview?

But I haven't worked for a year, and I have another time gap in my résumé. How do I handle that?

So what? Where is it written that everyone must be continuously employed—from graduation to who knows what?

Do not be afraid of questions about the time you spent away from work. Answer honestly and forthrightly: "I was raising children"; "I went to school"; "I grew vegetables"; "I loafed." But whatever you did during that time, present it as a positive experience—that's what is important. The difference between "loafing" and using the time to "explore the city, read the classics, and fill in the gaps in my education" can mean the difference between interest and apathy on the part of the interviewer.

Don't be ashamed. Stand up and tell them what you learned.

Should I adopt a "wait and see" attitude after an interview?

First off, come home and send a follow-up letter. Thank the interviewer for the time spent with you and the knowledge gained about the workings of the company, and express your continued interest in the position—if that's the case. Send it immediately, while you're still fresh in the interviewer's mind; and send it on your personal stationery or plain white paper—your present company letterhead is a no-no.

Keep track of the people you talk to, résumés you send (index cards are perfect for this task). After a reasonable time, one or two weeks, make a follow-up phone call to find out the status of the decision. Request a realistic assessment of your chances—you deserve it—and then decide whether to keep it as an open option or move on to something else.

I followed your suggestions about communicating more informally, and now my clients are questioning the new me. How do I handle this?

Good for you—you're making an impact! Tell them what you have learned; tell them why you've come to realize that communication is the name of the game; and ask for feedback.

I tried your suggestions—and they backfired—what do I do now?

Keep at it; try again. Maybe the presentation method wasn't right for the situation, or maybe the people weren't right, or maybe you weren't right. Modify the presentation—but keep on trying.

I tried your suggestions, made an impact, and am getting results—can I spread the word?

Of course you can, and you should!

Let people know what you're doing; let them know you're willing and eager to do a little more than what is expected. Don't hide in your office—come out and show them what you can do. And in doing that, you'll show others how they can grow as well.

The more you promote yourself, the more you let people

in on what you have learned and what you're doing, the better you will feel about yourself—and the better they will feel about themselves.

So share your insights with others—that's communication and that's making an impact!

About the Author

Caryl Winter is a specialist in business communications. She brings her experiences in the corporate world to her teaching position at UCLA's Division of Business and Management, and conducts workshops and seminars on the art of business writing, making effective presentations, and developing policies and procedures. A former New Yorker, Ms. Winter now lives with her husband in Los Angeles.

PLANNING YOUR CAREER
from
BEGINNING TO END...
from
Ballantine Books